D1235573

The Compassionate Community

CATHERINE M. HARMER

THE COMPASSIONATE COMMUNITY

Strategies That Work for the Third Millennium

Wipf & Stock
PUBLISHERS
Eugene, Oregon

Grateful acknowledgment is made to the following for permission to reprint copyrighted material: "The Beatitudes" © 1968 by Medical Mission Sisters; *Scripture Readings: Featuring All-Inclusive Language* © 1989 by the Carmelites of Indianapolis, for all scripture quotes, unless otherwise indicated. Translations of scripture from the *New Revised Standard Version of the Bible* © 1989 by the Division of Christian Education of the National Council of Churches of Christ in the USA. Used by permission. All rights reserved.

Wipf and Stock Publishers
199 W 8th Ave, Suite 3
Eugene, OR 97401

The Compassionate Community
Strategies that Work for the Third Millennium
By Harmer, Catherine M.
Copyright©1998 Orbis Books
ISBN: 1-59752-046-2
Publication date 1/11/2005
Previously published by Orbis Books, 1998

This work is dedicated to a number of people.

First, it is dedicated to those women and men from all walks of life, all religions, all ethnic and national groups, who have seen the suffering of the people and who have responded in whatever way was within their power. These are people in churches, in business, in education, in government, in healthcare—those who work publicly and those who work privately. It is dedicated to those who provide ideas, time, energy, and caring action. May they continue to reach out as people of justice, compassion, and community.

It is dedicated very specially to those who are the sufferers in our world, the young and the old, the healthy and the sick, those who still struggle and those who have given up in despair. To them is extended the hope that their suffering has not been in vain, and that the future will be better for them.

Finally, it is dedicated to the new generations of people, not yet on this earth, in the hope that their lives will be better because of what people of good will, of compassion and community, are doing and will be doing to create a better world for everyone.

CONTENTS

PROLOGUE

Happy are the poor, they shall inherit the land.
Happy those who know what sorrow means, they shall understand.
Happy those who hold no claims, we'll put the world into their hand.
Happy those who hunger and thirst for goodness, for they shall be satisfied.
Happy are you who dare to think and do, who dare to have tried.

Happy are the merciful, they shall have mercy in return.
Happy are the utterly sincere, God is their sole concern.
Happy those who die for peace, they die that all of us may learn.
Happy those who suffer the scourge of hatred, whose freedom is denied.
Happy are you who dare to think and do, who dare to have died.

Happy is the one who has learned to handle blame.
Happy those who are ill-treated for the glory of my name,
For in this and every age, we treat the prophets just the same.
So I say be glad, you my friends, and thankful, for great is your reward.
Happy are you who dare to think and do, and be like the Lord.

—"Beatitudes," by Sr. Miriam Therese Winter

INTRODUCTION

"Whatsoever you do to the least of my people, you do to me."
(Matthew 25:40)

A few years ago I came out of a cathedral in a major city with a group of people representing church personnel. We had spent days talking about those who dedicate their lives to the works of the church. The Mass had been about the gospel values to which everyone in that group would and could say "Amen" and mean it.

As we came down the steps, a homeless man was standing there. He was dirty and ragged, and he held out a styrofoam cup, asking for money. People ahead of me looked the other way, no doubt embarrassed. He caught my eye and I could not look away. I took a dollar out of my purse and gave it to him, saying, "Get something to eat, brother."

From the cathedral we went back to the hotel for supper. I was shaken by the encounter. I knew all the stuff about homelessness that was commonly said. In my heart I was pretty sure he would use that money for drink rather than food. Nevertheless, my heart was moved and I could not pass by. I believe that what I experienced at that moment was compassion, "suffering with." None of the rational sides of my mind could function. All I could do was to give him what he asked for.

It would have been much better if I could have gotten him into a shelter, found him a job, reunited him with his family. I could not. So I did what I could in that moment. What I also did, however, was to begin to look into the whole question of homelessness: its causes, the efforts being made to combat it, and steps being taken to help the sufferers. What I came to see was that most of what was being done was not very helpful to the homeless. Shelters were a stopgap that in fact kept people homeless. Since they had to line up by mid-afternoon to get in, they couldn't get jobs or keep their children in school—if these children could even get into school.

The nightly television news is always in some sense a source of distress. After news bytes about child abuse, drive-by shootings, and burned-out buildings in the inner city, we watch ads that tell us how to keep our skin young looking, reduce our waist line, grow new hair, or thicken what we have. A story on homelessness is followed by a pitch for the newest and latest high priced luxury car. The endless juxtaposition of the awful and the foolish can deaden our senses or even lead to a feeling of despair.

Our politicians talk to us about balanced budgets, national security priorities, and billions of dollars in programs for military spending. We hear of the need to reduce money spent on welfare, knowing that some money protected by the government is welfare for the rich. While the subsidy to the pregnant unmarried teenager is denied, the subsidy to the tobacco industry is protected.

Out of another reality, the religious one we claim as part of our heritage, we believe it is important to protect the young, the weak, the elderly, the poor. Jesus said: "Suffer the little children to come to me." Yet we have little children being denied healthcare, food, and housing in the name of national security or balanced budgets. Does the Statue of Liberty really say: "Send me your poor..."? And if it does, why is that barbed wire wall going up along our southern border?

We are caught up in a new world where some of our cherished values have been suspended. My generation was born during the "Great Depression" and many became part of the "Great Society." We believed that if we studied and worked hard, did our part, we would succeed. Now some of my contemporaries look at the poor, the unemployed, the homeless, and say with conviction that if "those people" wanted to, they could make it too. What has been forgotten is that the children of the thirties came out on top at the cost of a major world war which, in the weird reality of the times, meant an end to the Depression and the start of good times for many people in America.

Something else came out of that depression period. When Franklin D. Roosevelt came to the presidency in 1933, he won on the promises he had made to get the country moving again. The massive social programs initiated over the following years did more than simply put into place social security and the many safety systems that were aimed at getting the country moving and providing security for the elderly, children, and the temporarily unemployed. More significant was the incredible redefinition of *community*. Roosevelt created the concept of *the whole country as one community*, of people being responsible one for another. This sense of one community was reinforced by the united effort during World War II. The spirit of pulling together, of helping one another and so helping the world, was of the essence of that time.

Over the years, that sense of community has shrunk to the size of one's state or city or neighborhood; now, for many, it is so small as to be limited to family and friends. Taking care of one's own can be accompanied by a turning of one's back, not only on the values of a nation, but also on the deeper values that go beyond any nation. Those deeper values cut across nations, across religions, across races. Fundamental to those values is *compassion*, the ability to suffer with others, to have one's heart touched to the point of wanting to do something to relieve that suffering.

A few years after my encounter with the homeless man outside the cathedral, I was working with a religious congregation in the Pacific Northwest which had been trying to deal with homelessness in their city. They had gone from working in temporary shelters, to establishing a small house for homeless women, and finally to developing and opening a long-term residential facility for homeless women and children. This facility provides small apartments, training for the mothers, day care for the pre-school children, and after school programs, as well as a host of training experiences to move the families forward. At an assembly of the sisters, some of the women then in the facility spoke about the experiences which had changed their lives and those of their children. Suddenly, I found myself back on the steps of the cathedral with that man and his styrofoam cup. Here was a strategy that worked instead of my strategy that had not!

This book is about that man and those women, and about a lot of other people who in our country and in many countries around the world are in the dangerous situation of trying to live and to do the highwire act of survival without a safety net. It is about what has happened because compassion seems to have died out in whole sections of our contemporary society. It is about the need to revive an understanding of community that is bigger than the immediate family or even the neighborhood. It is about one who said: "Whatsoever you did to the least of my people, you did to me" (Mt 25:40).

It is about a whole host of social problems that exist all around us, social problems afflicting real people: the hungry, the unemployed, the victims of crime and violence, those without shelter, the elderly who are fearful of needing to choose between medicine and food or heat. It is about children in schools that do not teach even the basics and that, after twelve years, turn them out as adult illiterates.

This book is about the failed strategies of the past. The solution to crime, we have been told, is to have more police on the streets and more prisons, and yet while the crime rate is going down the prison population is going up. The solution to teenage pregnancy is to deny welfare to the mother and her children. Yet, in states that have refused funding for additional children born to unwed teenagers, the state-funded abortion rate is rising. The solution to homelessness is more shelters or jail, though "not in my neighborhood." The welfare system is said to be ineffective and destructive of families. The solution: make them go to work, even though poor education and low skills limit their job potential, and the salaries they receive will not provide enough to live on, or to afford safe child care.

One night, listening to one of our Congressional leaders talking about orphanages and workhouses for the poor, I found myself raging: "Doesn't he know that these things do not work?" Perhaps he doesn't. Or perhaps he does, but does not care. There is a growing sense that government's goal is to protect the wealthy while the rest must take care of themselves. Supply-side economics, a "trickle down" theory, claims that as the rich get richer, some of it will trickle down to the rest. We know from experience that it does not work.

The morning after my raging at the Congressman, I decided to look for strategies that could work to make the changes we need so badly in our world today. That decision led to this book and started me on a wonderful journey of discovery. I found myself moving beyond the borders of America to some very creative ideas in Bangladesh, in Ghana, in Peru, and many other places. We have much to learn from the so-called Third World or, better, the Two-Thirds World. What was so overpowering as I looked at these strategies was how simple they are, how local, and how independent of large bureaucracies. These strategies that work can be done in different ways by different people. There can be a place in these strategies for everyone to be part of the solution instead of the problem.

What we need to reclaim are the three essentially *human* elements of compassion, community, and justice. By doing so, we can commit ourselves, and we can find a renewed understanding of what Jesus meant in the Beatitudes, what Mohammed meant in the Koran, what Isaiah spoke of in the Hebrew Testament. We might find the courage to do whatever is needed. We might find that we do not have to choose between looking away from the homeless man with his styrofoam cup or putting a dollar in it. We might even find that we can help to make a difference that will last. If we do, then we will not have lived in vain.

PART I

THE SITUATION

CHAPTER 1

The Call to Compassion

"Blessed are the merciful, for they shall obtain mercy."
(Matthew 5:7)

To be compassionate means to be among the merciful ones, those whom Jesus blessed in the Beatitudes. Jesus promised that because they were merciful they too would be the recipients of mercy. The importance of compassion or mercy cannot be overestimated. An individual who is without compassion is cold, hard, unfeeling. Such a person cannot feel with others, or understand what is happening within them or to them. To be without compassion is to carry self-centeredness and selfishness to an extreme. It is compassion which makes it possible to come in touch with the other, to *feel with* the other. Compassion involves the ability to imagine the reality and situation of the other.

Movies, television, and now virtual reality computers can touch the imagination, and thus the feelings, at a deep level. It is possible to watch a play and be moved to tears by the final words of a Joan of Arc about to enter into a fiery death. Exposure to the pain and suffering of the other can have another side, however, which is that we can become hardened to the things we see and shut them out. During the Vietnam War the daily television news broadcasts showing the suffering of children mobilized some people into anti-war action or relief efforts. The same broadcasts closed other people's minds and hearts to the reality, even to the point of denial. It was possible to treat it like a movie. It was even possible to watch these scenes nightly and believe that the death of a child from napalming was essential to our national security, and in any case—she was probably Viet Cong!

COMPASSION AND JUSTICE

It is important to see the connection between compassion and justice, to know that without compassion it is impossible to live justly. It is very important to recover a sense of passion and to recognize it as basic to any sense of morality and justice. Compassion is at the core of true justice.

If we find ourselves looking at the suffering around us and concluding it is all "their own fault," and if we are comfortable listening to politicians talking about balancing budgets on the backs of the poor, it may be that we have lost not only our sense of compassion, but also our sense of justice. We hear good people expressing sentiments such as, "Why should the hard-earned money of the working people support those who are lazy?" What is frightening is not only that such statements are based on faulty information, but also that we are talking about *other human beings*, about people who are suffering, children and the elderly, women and men, and we are talking about them as if they were not human beings just like us. We have created a chasm between ourselves and those who suffer.

The call to be just is not a matter of choice but rather of responsibility. It is a call to what is basic to our humanity. While frequently supported and called for by religious systems, justice itself is of the nature of humanity. Even the child recognizes what is "fair" or "unfair" and rails against those things perceived as unjust. When we speak of having a *right* to something, we are calling upon justice.

Today, we see in action a reality that was noted in another time by the great moral theologian Reinhold Niebuhr who believed that what made it easier for us to be inhumane to one another was our tendency to establish a "we-they" dichotomy. If we see ourselves in one reality and the others, the "they," as somehow opposite and possibly antithetical to our good, it is much easier to take very inhumane stances. If the pregnant teenage mother and her child are viewed as "they," as the other over there who threatens the welfare of our children over here, it becomes easier to talk of cutting off benefits to that mother and her child. This is the element of distancing oneself, of looking the other way and blaming the victim so that, as a result, these people become less real. We are like children playing cops and robbers, shooting one another, assuming that when the game is over everyone will get up and walk away. This is a failure of imagination, of rationality, of compassion and, in the end, a failure of justice. Not only the mother and her child suffer. We also suffer for having lost compassion and justice. As a result we become less than human.

CENTRALITY OF COMMUNITY

Another reality that is both developing and dying simultaneously in our world, especially in the Western world, is the desire for community. We have seldom seen a time in our history when there was more emphasis on the *idea* of community and the yearning for it. Nevertheless, we also live in an age when the realities and the demands of community are less well understood and are, therefore, increasingly neglected. America was founded by communities and has for much of its history been a nation of communities. Today, a hunger for community sends people searching in workshops, communes, churches, neighborhoods, schools, even health clubs. Too often the hunger is not met, because the reality of community, of "being in union with," is overpowered by the personal need for self-protection.

To be a community means to be united and to be committed to the payment of the costs of that unity. It means being available to give support as well as being able to find it. There is a mutuality in community that requires both giving and receiving. No community can exist without understanding and compassion. When Franklin Delano Roosevelt helped to create a sense that the whole nation was a community, the need was so great, the devastation of the Depression so total, that people were able to respond. Roosevelt was able to speak to the minds and hearts of a paralyzed people and call them forth to help themselves and one another. The basic values and beliefs of America were touched very deeply, both by the Depression and by the call to move together as a community to change it. The current emphasis on dismantling the specific programs that came out of that effort has led to a denigration of the *spirit* of the American people.

In the last few years of the twentieth century, we can trace the weakening of a sense of community to a number of factors. There is clearly a growing loss of trust in the public part of life, that world outside of the intimate community of family and home. It is fed by the fear of crime which leads to a distrust of the stranger, including those different from us even if they live on the same street. Trust is further undermined by the frustration with public officials, politicians, the political system in general, all of which are frequently viewed as self-serving rather than community-serving. The increasingly negative aspects of political campaigning in the last twenty-five years have led many to feel that those running for political office are more interested in winning the office, regardless of cost in money or truth, than they are in working for the betterment of the country, its people, and the larger world.

Robert Theobald calls the coming age the "compassionate era," believing that it will be built primarily on trust and relationships. At times it is difficult to *see* any such movement. Yet, in a variety of ways large numbers of people are in fact working toward and creating this compassionate era. They are doing it through individual and group efforts, neighborhood organizations, churches, civic and professional groups. The seeds are planted deeply in human culture but need to be nurtured, especially at a time when compassion and community are under threat from a self-serving segment of the population.

We may be moving into an important stage in human history. Necessity has created opportunities to develop a new civil reality, one in which people respond to the needs of others out of a realization that the good of the many is connected to their own good. Many people write and speak of the value of the "good society" which combines the goodness of the individual with a public sense for good laws. We see examples of people who have experienced an inner transformation as they reach out to help others in need. Volunteer groups are a living testament to the fact that if we are caring persons we help ourselves as much if not more than those to whom we reach out.

Many of today's societal structures are not functioning well. Our schools seem unable to educate. Our churches often provide for spiritual needs only at a very superficial and formalized level. Families are "nuclear" now in a way that makes growing up a very dangerous and difficult experience for far too many children. The coming age may require new structures to replace some of those which no longer serve the common good. If we are going to attempt to develop such structures, we will need to trust the people who have the interest and the ability to try new concepts and new action plans. We will need to be open to new types of partnerships based on being honest in terms of what we need and being courageous in moving forward.

Compassion may be what is needed to bring about a renewal of the *communitarian* elements so needed today. The excesses which are spawned by a politics that puts an undue emphasis on individualism need to be juxtaposed with a revival of an earlier tradition of covenant and civic virtue. In the rebirth of a sense of community there could re-emerge a more humane political order. Too often we think of politics as something that happens every few years, rather than as one of the central modes by which our life is bettered or worsened. Our political system, like the other systems in our world, needs to be converted to a more compassionate and community-centered reality.

The sense of belonging to one another is at the heart of any true community. It is not possible, for any good and sane person at least, to turn away from those who belong to us. If we see public life, society, the civic reality as a type of mutual belonging, then it is much harder to turn our backs on some parts of that public, of that community. This spirit of belonging is still found in some parts of the world. Most often it is found in small communities of neighbors, or in religious groups. It is this sense of belonging which has been lost, tragically, in the decades of "me-ism," of corporate raiders, of economic downsizing, and of ethnic, racial, and other forms of violence by some against others.

The compassionate community acting justly is clearly needed in our present world and is essential if we are to deal with the many dysfunctions of that world. It is the compassionate and just community which will make our journey into the coming century and into the third millennium a step forward rather than simply a turning of a page on the calendar.

CHAPTER 2

Religions and the Compassionate Way

"Be compassionate as God is compassionate."
(Luke 6:36)

All the great religious traditions speak of the values of the individual and the community, the virtues of mercy and compassion, and the interconnections of public and private experience. However, in every tradition there has been an erosion of the life and vigor of the original vision and belief. Modern emphases on economic power, political dominance, and individual against group have drained some spiritual energy from all of the traditions. In some cases, the leaders of the religions have been co-opted by political or economic powers.

A fundamentalist understanding of religious reality has struck at the basic roots of religion itself. Extreme right-wing Christianity denies or limits the key and central teaching of Jesus, so that "Love one another as I have loved you" is not preached. Rather, we hear about morals and vengeance, topics that are somewhat distant from the Jesus who walked among the people, healing the sick, feeding the hungry, forgiving those caught in adultery, teaching the new law of love. Within some of the most conservative Jewish groups there is a belief that the goods of this world, wealth and security, are a reward from God and that poverty and misfortune are punishments for evil. Jesus met this same type of belief among the first-century Pharisees who could ask him, of the man born blind, "Who sinned? This man or his parents?"

Social religion is not the same as the religion of a society. Each of the religious communities must witness to its deepest values as a way of renewing and revitalizing a world that has lost its way or perhaps sold its birthright for a mess of potage. The churches need to maintain the integrity of the vision, to act and express themselves publicly in a manner which is authentic. The great depth of understanding that religion can bring to the world will be lost unless the religions *act* out of their vision and wisdom. If any age has ever needed a deep spirituality to inform its reality and shape its actions, it is the present one. There will always be a tension between religion and the civic life; the challenge to religion is to resist becoming the tool of the society, to remain its challenger. We look to religion to help us understand the human reality, both individual and communal.

A rediscovery of the wealth of the spiritual culture which is basic to all religions can help us come to a renewed sense of a compassionate and just community. Religion can serve to remind us that the most important elements of this life, in this world, are deeply connected to something greater than this world. Regardless of the words we use, the names we give to divinity, the rules we follow, the theology we formulate, there is something we share that is beyond any of us. It is in coming in touch with this deeper reality that we begin to create a solid base for a compassionate, humane community that acts justly.

THE BIBLICAL TRADITION

The biblical tradition is in strong contrast to the lack of compassion. The Hebrew and Christian scriptures speak constantly of the importance of caring for the poor, the suffering, widows, children, the sick. For Jesus, compassion was the central quality in the life of anyone centered in God. The evangelist Luke (6:36) quotes Jesus as saying: "Be compassionate as God is compassionate," thus emphasizing that Jesus' message is about a way of life grounded in an imitation of God. This imitation of God goes beyond the rational mode and focuses on the importance of feeling the suffering of others so that we are moved to do something to alleviate it. To *feel* compassion leads us to *be compassionate* in action.

Jesus tells the story of the priest and the Levite who passed by the man lying injured on the road to Jericho. The Samaritan was the one who bound up his wounds, took him to an inn, and paid for his care. Jesus holds up as an example the one who was compassionate, who did not turn away. According to Jesus, the community that turns away from its neediest risks God's displeasure. The Hebrew scriptures claim the poor as those under the eye of God and warn: "Those who oppress the poor insult their Maker, but those who are kind to the needy honor God" (Prov 14:31, NRSV).

In both the Hebrew and the Christian scriptures, the spirit of God calls for true righteousness, demanding much more than simple justice, requiring a deep and compassionate response. In spite of these calls in the scriptures, the followers of both Judaism and Christianity have often fallen short of what God demands. It is one thing to fail to live up to what one believes, as an individual and as a society. It is much worse to know what is demanded and to subvert that call by preaching a message of uncompassionate, uncaring oppression of the poor.

Liberation theology speaks of the option for the poor, stressing that God has a *preferential* stance toward the poor, the neglected, the deprived, and those against whom the righteous sin. In declaring his mission, Jesus spoke directly to the reality of the poor and to what those who claim to follow him must do. He took to himself, as a definition of his mission, the words of Isaiah: "The Spirit of God is upon me, because God has anointed me to preach good news to the poor. God has sent me to proclaim release to the captives, recovery of sight to the blind, to set at liberty those who are oppressed, to proclaim the acceptable year of God" (Lk 4:18-19). The "year of God" is the year of Jubilee, the fiftieth year, which will come again in the year 2000, the millennial year.

OTHER RELIGIOUS TRADITIONS

Islam, founded after both Judaism and Christianity, takes from both many of its own teachings and tenets. It is the third of the

great religions of "The Book." Just as many of the teachings of
Judaism are related to the socio-political realities of the times
in which the Old Testament was developing, so too the teachings of Islam reflect the cultural realities of the period in which
the Koran was written. Judaism, Christianity, and Islam have
much in common. All three emphasize the basic connection
between serving God and serving others and all three recognize the need for and require compassion.

The Islamic tradition contains the concept of *zakat*, the
obligation of helping the poor and the suffering (Koran,
22:41). The followers of Mohammed are required to strive for
the good of all humanity, for the growth and development of
all peoples. *Zakat* is connected essentially to *salat*, the service of
God. In Islam it is not possible to serve God without serving
others. *Zakat* is not simply a personal obligation, but also a
communal one, a collective responsibility. The interaction of
the individual and the community in Islam makes it possible to
carry out the obligations of membership in that faith.

The Koran speaks of compassion, as does the Bible. In
defining what constitutes piety, the Koran states:

> Piety lies in believing in God, the last day and the an-
> gels, and Scriptures and the prophets, and disbursing
> your wealth out of love for God, among your kin and
> the orphans, the wayfarers and mendicants, freeing
> the slaves, observing your devotional obligations, and
> in paying the zakat and fulfilling a pledge you have
> given, and being patient in hardship, adversity, and
> times of peril. (Koran: 2:177)

The Koran, like the Bible, speaks directly of the obligation
toward the alien, the immigrant, the refugee. It is important to
keep this in mind when discussing immigration and refugees in
Europe and North America. The issue is not simply political or
economic. As the three major Western religions make clear,
the response to the reality of immigrants and refugees must include an underlying religious and spiritual dimension which
transcends politics and economics and draws people to a higher call and a greater demand.

The Western world, Europe and the Americas, has been benefiting from the expansion of a number of other great religious traditions. Hinduism and Buddhism are no longer exotic religions only studied in comparative religion courses. We find ashrams and monasteries in many countries. Those who practice these two religions are made aware of the strong traditions of care and concern for the poor and the oppressed. In our century we have witnessed the examples of Mohandas Gandhi and the Dalai Lama speaking out for the needs of the poor, the dispossessed, the suffering. Mohandas Gandhi wrote, spoke, and demonstrated the law of love as the basic law of humanity. The doctrine of *ahimsa*, non-violence, flows from the centrality of love. Gandhi preached that the law of love is equivalent to the law of life. His belief in the importance of love was based in his Hindu background, and grew as a result of his reading and study of Christianity. As he stood against the British Raj in India and the racism of South Africa, he constantly reminded the leaders of those Christian countries of the message of Jesus!

Turning away from those who suffer, from the poor and oppressed, is a form of violence even if one never raises a hand or a voice. Cutting off funds from needy mothers and children, denying essential assistance to the elderly, refusing healthcare to those without insurance ... these are all forms of violence.

Buddhism, an ancient religion, is very much alive today in many parts of the world quite distant from the places in which it originated. It is a way of living, not simply a collection of tenets or proscriptions. Compassion is one of the elements found both in the ancient and the modern writings of Buddhist scholars and in the lives of holy people. According to Buddhist teachings, compassion cannot simply be theory but needs to be enfleshed in practical action directed toward the alleviation of suffering. Compassion is not true compassion unless it is active. Buddhist monasticism combines the depth of a life of intense prayer with an openness to being a healing and helping presence in society. Like the Christian monks of the Middle Ages, Buddhist monks view as inconceivable the possibility of living a life of prayer and contemplation without being open to the neighbor, the migrant, the poor, and the dispossessed.

What all these religions proclaim in one way or another is that it is not enough to speak and think of compassion. Beautiful words and statements will not replace the action needed. To give lip service to compassion and then allow oneself to act without compassion is to violate the deepest beliefs and values of Judaism, Christianity, Islam, Hinduism, and Buddhism.

So much of the dread of the poor, the hatred of the refugee and immigrant, the heartless treatment of the oppressed, is based on fear. When we look at the homeless man begging outside the church door, the homeless woman pushing her cart along our city streets, we see what we could and might be. The fear that underlies many of the things we say is that we too could become poor, homeless, outcast. Too often, the adherents of any religion use religion as a way of assuring themselves that all is well with them. They are doing what is asked, they work hard, they are good to their children. Yet, when we go back to the true teachings of all the great religions, we find that there is a reminder that suffering people are around us, and that it is important not to look away, not to turn our backs on the poor, the widow, the orphan, the alien...but rather to move toward them in love and compassion, in works of justice and charity, lifting their burdens, sharing our goods and our very selves. Rather than fearing that if we share there will not be enough for ourselves, we are assured that to the degree that we reach out to others, so will we be cared for.

What we are being asked to be, by all of our religions, by all of our theologies, can be captured in the one call of Jesus to all of us, an immensely simple and yet incredibly difficult call:

Be compassionate as God is compassionate. (Luke 6:36)

CHAPTER 3

Justice within the Compassionate Community

*"God has showed you, my people, what is good; and
what does God require of you but to do justice, and to
love kindness, and to walk humbly with your God?"*
(Micah 6:8)

As a child in grade school, both in the public kinder-
garten and later in the Catholic grades, I, like most
American children, started the day by standing and
solemnly intoning: "I pledge allegiance to the flag of the United States of America and to the Republic for which it stands,
one nation, under God, indivisible, with liberty and justice for
all." I suspect that most of us, if we had been asked to explain
the last phrase, would have had little difficulty with the word
liberty but might have had more trouble with the word justice.
Many years later, as a Medical Mission Sister, I heard our
foundress, Anna Dengel, on more than one occasion say with
great emphasis about the medical mission work to which we
were committed around the world, "Sisters, our work is not a
work of charity. It is a work of justice." It was a long time before
I fully understood the distinction that she was making.

Often we find good people who are engaged in very noble
and fine works of charity. The "Lady Bountiful" legend is one
which was dear to us as children. The great miracles of Jesus—
his curing of the sick and raising of the dead—we often think

of as works of charity. Yet, when we think about the words *chari-ty* and *justice*, we realize that each has a different feel. So often when we think of charity, what comes to mind are works of kindness that flow out of our abundance, either of goods or of fine feeling. These works are things we are not obliged to do, but which we do because we are moved. Sometimes this is how we see the outcomes of compassion. Having been moved by the suffering of others, we do a work of charity. That means we do something not demanded of us.

Justice is something else, something before the charitable. What Anna Dengel meant was that the works of healing were not charity because people have a *right* to good health and to assistance in times of ill health. To feed the hungry is to give them what is rightfully theirs. In the American dream we speak of "life, liberty, and the pursuit of happiness" as *rights* that people have. One cannot have these if one does not have food, housing, health, work, and education. A just society is one which recognizes certain basic rights and in justice sees that they are shared by all. People often look upon the welfare system as some kind of fund which can be continued or cut off, since it is a form of state charity. In fact, it is one of the ways in which the state meets its obligations of justice to its people.

Individuals too have an obligation of justice. To act justly is a characteristic of the good person as well as the good society. The just person is concerned not only about the immediate community of family, but also about the larger community, which can extend to the whole world. The challenge is to live justly. One is concerned about the poor, about orphans, widows, and the sick, because justice demands it. Charity, whether we admit it or not, has an element of doing something *if we are able*, or out of the goodness of our heart, if we have the spare time or extra money. Justice, on the other hand, requires us to do all that we can no matter the cost. Not every person or group can challenge me to justice, but those which can do so cannot be denied.

As an essential part of the good life, justice is therefore the concern and responsibility of each and every one of us. Justice is a personal call, based in human virtue, but it is also a necessary quality in good institutions, in good systems, and in good government. If we are not just in our lives and in our actions, if we do not have just systems, if our government does not function with justice "toward all," then charity becomes the necessary band-aid, the fix-it, that which tries to make up for the basically *unjust* reality of the world around us.

Throughout human history, there have been times when justice has been so weak that the role of charity has become essential. Often it was the charity of churches, of benevolent societies, of good persons, which tried to make up for the injustices of government and of the commercial world. The difficulty is that charity alone cannot make up for large-scale injustice. What frequently happened was that poverty was tended to by the charitable institutions with no demand made on the systems which, through their injustice, had created the situations of poverty. The Industrial Revolution brought with it huge jumps forward in terms of progress, but at the cost of grave injustices to women, to children, to workers in factories. The owners of factories built their businesses and their personal wealth—even the progress of their nations—through incredibly unjust treatment of workers. It was these injustices in industry that gave birth to the labor movement and unions. The cry of the unions was for justice, not charity!

Justice and compassion move together. We turn a blind eye to injustice when we are unable to feel compassion. Many people knew of and saw the horrendous conditions of child labor in nineteenth-century England. Charles Dickens was moved by compassion and in his novels, published as serials in newspapers, made the horrors of child labor real to many people who otherwise were able to look the other way. We can tolerate injustices by insisting to ourselves that "they like it that way," or "they are different from us," or "they don't feel things the way we do." We distance ourselves by falling into a "we" versus "they" mentality. Regardless of how we rationalize, we are supporting injustice.

When exercising charity, we tend to choose among many good efforts, and so we support the homeless, or the sufferers of a particular disease or disorder. When exercising justice, however, we must be concerned for the whole community. Thus, in talking about the various approaches to welfare reform (an incredible euphemism for protecting the wealthy at the cost of the poor), we must be concerned for the entire community and all of its parts. If there is injustice in any part, then it affects all in some way or other. The injustice must be faced. We need to address the systems and institutions which, through their basic injustice, are creating the victims, the sufferers. We need also to be concerned about those who perpetrate the injustice, because they are also suffering the results of their actions, even if they are unaware of how much they have been diminished by their choices.

Justice and charity have to go hand in hand. Justice without charity can be cold and unfeeling. Charity without justice will be unable to reach all who suffer. Individuals, society, government, various systems—all need to be both just and charitable. It would be naive to think that when we have a totally just society there will be no problems. There will always be problems because of the ever-present reality of the failure of personal as well as communal responsibility. We are now in an era of very high levels of *societal* irresponsibility in the realm of justice, so it is not surprising that we also have high levels of personal irresponsibility expressed in crimes of all types, corporate and individual.

What we need now are social structures which can help to create the kind of society in which there is justice for all, and in which the poor are treated as an integral part of society. What we need is systemic change which affects all of the institutions of our society so that all the members are able to share in the good life.

THE MODERN SITUATION

As we look around us today we find a society of multiple contradictions. On the one hand, we like to think of ourselves as good people, caring people who are concerned about the whole as well as our own part of it. On the other hand, we are able to hear—and at times say—things that contradict our ideal picture of ourselves as individuals and as a group. A favorite place to visit in America is the Statue of Liberty. We read the inscription, we see the torch raised high, and our hearts are moved. We feel proud of our country and its history. Yet, on the very boat that takes us out to the statue, we may find ourselves looking with annoyance at some of the other people riding with us because they are a different color, or they speak a language we don't understand, or they dress in foreign-looking clothes.

Even those who do not stand outside the homes of newcomers, shouting for them to get out because they are different and their presence will lower property values, may find themselves in sympathy with their angry neighbors. From calls to deny healthcare to illegal immigrants, or welfare benefits to legal immigrants, to more measured demands to limit all immigration, there is a growing movement away from what has, in the past, been a source of pride for Americans. We all came out of an immigrant population, and we point with pride to how our ancestors, or perhaps our parents, made it in America.

People born in the Depression years may now view poverty as a crime of the poor rather than the result of a system which increasingly works for some people and against others, particularly against the poorest, the weakest, the most vulnerable. The same economic realities are being played out over and over in many parts of our world. The social democracies of Europe are moving away from caring for the poor and the deprived, and they are turning their backs on those who are new in their countries. The former Soviet empire, having taken on Western-style capitalism, is now turning its back on the elderly, the poor, and even the young who no longer have any sense of being protected by their government. The people who were the power elite in the old system have adjusted to the new and are as powerful and well off as in the past; the only difference is that the safety net has been removed from the others.

We are in an era when we are turning our backs, not only on the systems and the methods that helped the neediest, but also on the values and beliefs which made us proud of who we are and what we do as nations and people. The shift into a super-individualism is bringing with it a cultural devastation as terrible as the economic one.

America from its very beginnings was a place of immigrants, sometimes called colonists, who fled various kinds of persecution: religious, political, and economic. The first generations were clearly illegal immigrants, since the people already living in what is now North, Central, and South America were not asked if they wished to admit these newcomers. The people who lived here issued no visas. They were simply invaded and pushed out of the lands their people had inhabited for centuries.

What was very important to the colonists, for reasons of survival, was the reality of community. They had to help one another and be helped or they would not survive. Indeed, much of the help in the earliest years came from the very people whose land had been invaded, and who were later pushed out and even exterminated. Yet, while there was a strong community sense, there was also a heavy emphasis on individualism. These contrasting—often even conflicting—values are a part of the American heritage, as is the reality that we grabbed land and displaced a whole people. We need to recognize the tension between being a community, caring for all, and being individuals caring primarily for ourselves. Our country's history is grounded in the uncomfortable co-existence of two very different value systems which continue today. We are often fairly good at keeping the two in balance, but just as often we fail. Many people still believe that somehow if one takes care of oneself and one's family the benefits will reach everyone. Recently, on the news, I heard a man speaking of layoffs, and his comment was that while some people would lose jobs, that was all right because others would live better. In a way he was saying that some people need to die for the others, like the high priest Caiaphas who "was the one who had advised the Jews that it was better to have one person die for the people" (John 18:14, NRSV). In the case of Jesus, it was *his* choice to die for the people.

Adam Smith, to whom we are indebted for the philosophy behind "lean and mean," taught that individual self-interest would create social good, but he ignored the damage done to some by the self-interested action of others. We watch as businesses are downsized to save money in salaries and give investors an increased dividend, and as corporate executives are given millions of dollars in bonuses. We continue to be told that competition that hurts some people and helps the few will in some magical way end up helping everyone. These are people who could sell the Brooklyn Bridge! In companies which have huge losses, we find the very executives who so badly managed the company being given large bonuses while their workers are asked to take salary cuts or are laid off.

The endless arguments over the minimum wage witness to the illogic that underlies our injustice: we are willing to allow incredible benefits to some people while denying even the minimum needed to survive to others, specifically those we expect to provide us with services. The belief that all need to be of concern to us because they are part of our community comes under attack when individual self-interest overpowers our sense of obligation to one another and to the broader community. This is a daily failure of justice.

The basic injustice which is woven into the capitalist system has become so much a part of our reality that we lose sight of it until some really egregious example shocks us into awareness. Several years ago the American auto companies were in a very dangerous financial situation. They asked for great sacrifices from their workers, and the workers agreed. However, when things got better for the companies, the CEOs received large bonuses, but the workers did not get any reward for their sacrifices. They had to fight to get back even a portion of what they had given up.

One of the great myths of America is that of "boot straps." It comes out of our retelling of our pioneer history, starting with landing on Plymouth Rock and through the "conquest" of the west. In this myth, the strong individual pulls himself/herself up by the boot straps, unassisted by anyone else. What is often overlooked in this story is that so many of those individuals died in their efforts, and that those who succeeded did so because others came to their help, willingly or unwillingly. Nevertheless, the myth of rugged individualism has existed throughout our history, and it is still with us. The rugged individual today may be the corporate raider, who makes large quantities of money at the cost of destruction of companies, wide-scale unemployment through downsizing, and questionable, if not illegal, methods.

The society that is unjust to some part of itself ends up, eventually, paying for the injustice. History is filled with the stories of revolutions that came about when the injustices grew so blatant that people could no longer tolerate them. Our own revolution was based, at least in part, on unfair taxation. The French Revolution came about when the discrepancies between the majority who were poor and the few who were incredibly rich became so offensive that the people rose up in anger. No society can survive when the injustices become too great. America may come to a more just system, not because of its beliefs, but because the number of those who suffer the injustices is growing. A society faces a critical danger point when the so-called "middle class" begins to suffer the injustices of the rich. We may be closer to that point than we realize.

CHAPTER 4

The War on the Poor

"Blessed are the poor in spirit, for the realm of God is theirs."
(Matthew 5:3)

Americans have seen themselves at most times as a people who value compassion, community, and justice. In our history, we have had varied definitions for those three realities. During our earliest years, the sense of community was based on the fact of having been—whether as Pilgrims in New England, Quakers in Pennsylvania, or Catholics in Maryland—a people who had suffered together, who had emigrated together, and who were building a new life together. These people were conscious of the injustices that they had suffered, but except in the very early years, they were not so conscious of the injustices they were perpetrating on the peoples whose country they were taking over.

As the country grew, the degree of injustice to the Native Americans and to the slaves brought from Africa caused an erosion of the two foundational values of compassion and justice. So severe was the injustice in relation to slavery that it led to a great war that divided the country. The many wars of extermination against the Native Americans caused a chorus of voices to protest, but the protest was either too small or too soft to make a difference in the plans and actions of the government.

In spite of the harsh realities of our history, what has survived in the nation is a sense of the basic importance of the compassionate community that lives justly. Sometimes this sense survives only among a remnant. Nevertheless, at moments that touch the deepest myths of the people, these values resurface. When people began moving westward, the need for community was strong among those who were part of that trek. There were pioneer women who, while their men were subduing the Native Americans, were actively involved in learning from them and sharing much of what they knew with them.

Another recurring reality is that even when things become very bad, there have always been voices calling for justice, for compassion, and for true community. These voices spoke out against the "Indian wars," for safety and better working conditions for the women and children in the mills and factories of the nineteenth century, for civil rights for African Americans and women, and now for fair treatment of gays and lesbians. American history is a constant see-sawing between justice and privilege, community and individualism, compassion and self-serving.

WHO ARE THE POOR?

One of the prejudices brought to this country from England and other parts of the Western world was the denigration of the poor. Being poor was equated with being shiftless, lazy, amoral—if not immoral—and undependable. When members of the middle class fell on hard times, the concept of the "deserving poor" was used to allow them to be helped. Whether it was English landowners fencing off what had always been common land and putting people off farms, or factory owners imposing long hours, incredibly bad working conditions, and poor wages, the justification was that the poor needed to be controlled and that their natural vices of laziness, shiftlessness, and even crime needed to be kept in check. The great novels of Charles Dickens are filled with examples of the ability of otherwise good and religious people to compartmentalize their lives so that the suffering of the poor did not touch them.

In recent years many writers have addressed the growing movement in the U.S. toward a "lean and mean" approach to the poor. Rather than being the recipients of our concern, the poor are becoming the target of increasingly mean-spirited planning that worsens their plight. Welfare reform is spoken of in terms of helping the poor get work, catching welfare cheats, and balancing the federal budget. Once again it is a case of the haves deciding to protect what they have by denying even minimal assistance to the have-nots. We are watching government officials, who have sworn to protect the nation's people, determining that the way to protect the middle class, actually the wealthy, is to do it on the backs of the poorest, the weakest, and the most vulnerable.

One day, while he was president, Ronald Reagan held up a copy of the *New York Times* and announced on national television that anyone who wanted to work could do so. The paper, he noted, was full of jobs. I went out and got a copy of that day's paper. When I read through the want ads, I found many jobs for people with high levels of professional training: nurses, doctors, computer analysts, program developers, managers. There were a few jobs for waitresses, as well as some for fast food restaurants. I thought about some of the people I know who have no education beyond high school (and some have not even finished that), no training, and no experience. In an earlier time they would have worked in mills or in factories, none of which exist to any great extent in this country any longer. Few of the jobs listed that day would be open to them. I thought of women I know who are heading families because their husbands have died or walked away, and who can get only minimum wage jobs with no benefits—not even health benefits. They are on Aid to Families with Dependent Children (AFDC) because that way they can get health coverage for their children. It is hard to believe that anyone thinks it makes good sense to work at a fast food restaurant for minimum wage that will not cover child care, transportation to the job, and the other costs of surviving—such as health insurance—rather than accepting AFDC. Yet, we hear over and over again that they should get jobs, that they are shiftless!

That there are welfare cheats is true, though the number is less than 1 percent according to most research. That some people would rather not work is true. That welfare as we know it penalizes those who are married if the husband/father remains in the home is a sad commentary on where our values have gone. All this is true, but it is also only a part of the picture. What is most tragic is the suffering of so many: women, children, the elderly, working people, as well as those who want to work and cannot. What is as tragic is the death in America of the sense of compassion, of the belief that we are a community and that in a community people help one another, and the death of a sense of justice.

How just is it to deprive a woman of help for her children while we subsidize the tobacco industry? How just is it to keep the minimum wage well below the poverty level while giving tax breaks to the wealthiest people in the country and rewarding companies, again with tax breaks, who move their manufacturing to other countries, thus eliminating jobs? How just is it to deny basic healthcare to so many and then spend millions of dollars on organ transplants, which are so often merely new forms of medical experimentation. Ante-natal care for all the women in the U.S., we were told a few years ago, could be covered for ten years by simply building one less B1 bomber! Anyone in the health field knows that ante-natal care for women is one of the most cost effective aspects of healthcare. Ante-natal care costs very little in comparison with post-natal care for low-weight infants, who would probably have been full term normal weight children had their mothers received ante-natal care.

At some point along the way in recent years, the war on poverty declared by President Johnson turned into a war on the poor.

THE POLITICS OF COMPASSION

I often hear people say such things as, "Well that's politics for you!" And I find myself responding, "No, that's not politics." We have come to use the term *politics* as a synonym for self-serving sycophants who manage to hold power for themselves and their friends at the cost of the whole people. Yet *politics* comes from the Greek *polis* meaning "the people." We do not have to go all the way back to Plato to be told that to be in politics means to serve the good of the people. Over the last hundred years, the popes have written often of the rights of people and the obligations of governments.

Recently, theologians and others have begun to use the term "politics of compassion" as a paradigm for a new political order, a different kind of social system, one that would be communitarian and so balance the excesses generated by the dominant ethos of individualism. An overemphasis on the individual, on the one who can make it on his or her own, ignores the immense help that everyone gets during life. It also overlooks the reality that many of the people who have made it did so by the imposition of unjust methods and systems which took advantage of the poor, of workers, of women, and of minorities. The "politics of compassion" means a rediscovery of the concepts of *covenant* and of *civic virtue.* It is a reclaiming of the idea that we have covenants not simply with God, but also with one another, and that civic virtue means honoring that covenant.

A very important element of civic virtue is *benevolence,* the idea that all are involved in some way in service to the community, and that the activity is directed to heightening the well-being of the *community.* This goes beyond the idea of simply taking care of oneself and one's family. The members of the community have a *right* to call on one another for assistance when they cannot do something for themselves.

Perhaps more than anything else what we need today is a sense of transforming society. We have done much fixing, and patching, and adjusting over the years. What one congress puts into place another one changes or removes a few years later. The programs, plans, and strategies that we use may help for a while, but basically we need to transform the way we think, act, function, and decide. To transform our society will mean getting back in touch with the deepest values, the truest myths, the most energizing belief systems and working out of them.

To transform our society we will need to look at people, especially our poorest and most vulnerable, the way God looks at them. We will need to see all people not as "they" over against "us" but as "we." The community will be that of family, of neighborhood, of city, of country, and eventually of the world itself. Humanity cannot survive the endless wars, famines, brutality, and turning away from others that have so marked these final years of the second millennium. As we move into the third millennium, we can hope for something better, and we need to make sure that the something better is there for all of the people who make up the community of humanity.

PART II

STRATEGIES THAT WORK
AND THOSE THAT DO NOT

CHAPTER 5

Choice of Areas of Concern

"Defend the cause of the weak and the orphan;
maintain the rights of the poor and oppressed."
(Psalm 82:3)

In the world today we can find many areas of concern crying out for justice and compassion. When I began working on this book, I identified a dozen areas I might address. Gradually I narrowed down that number by applying three criteria. One criterion had to do with my own knowledge and experience, so that what I had to say would flow from actual contact with the situations analyzed. The second criterion was that the area be one that impacts the most vulnerable of our people. The third criterion was that the area represent not only an American situation, but a global one, so that both the realities and the solutions could be applicable beyond our limited borders.

With these criteria in mind, I have not attempted to deal with the immense area of crime, but rather with those aspects of crime which impact or involve women and children specifically. While I am absolutely convinced that a new economic order is necessary, I chose to look only at those parts of the economy that have the greatest role to play in alleviating the problems affecting many people. Healthcare is a wound crying out for major reform. Although healthcare concerns affect everyone, my focus here is on the most underserved, those who, because of poverty, age, or class, are deprived of even the basics needed for life to continue.

The great theoreticians often point the way to changes in entire systems, changes which I hope and believe will happen in the future, indeed, which must happen if we are to survive. While this book looks at the macro level of systemic change, it looks more intensively at the micro level, which is where change often begins. It is at the micro level where parts of systems are vulnerable to the pressures, the endeavors, the concerns of the ordinary people who are compassionate and just. Changes made at the micro level can begin a movement with the potential to change the macro level.

AREAS OF CONCERN

This book discusses strategies which can play a significant part in shaping a different world for the twenty-first century. I have chosen to focus on four major areas of immense concern and need. If we were to make significant changes in these alone, we would be a more compassionate and more just society, and many lives would be affected. The areas are: poverty as a dead end; homelessness; women and children at risk of violence; and inadequate healthcare for the poor. There is obvious overlap in these areas and I try to make the interconnections clear both in the reasons for the problems and the strategies that work to bring about change.

For each of the chosen areas, I lay out what I see to be the major problems for which there are presently very poor solutions. I define the background and the basis for the problem in a straightforward, simple—but hopefully not simplistic—way. I point out the present strategies which are clearly not working and explain why they are not working. Finally, for each area I identify strategies that do work. These are not just theoretical strategies; they are strategies which at present are being used successfully. In addition to describing the successful strategies, I introduce the real people who are working in actual programs that are making a difference and the real people who are being assisted out of the vicious cycle in which they have been caught.

Some of the programs that are described are small and local. Others are larger, national and even international. What they all have that brought them to my attention is the essence of community involvement, compassion and care, and a clear, if not always articulated, sense of justice. In the final analysis, I know that change is made by real people who are committed believers, who risk doing something small rather than waiting for the larger solutions. They are involved in strategies which, for the most part, do not depend on *big* government, though some do access funds from a variety of sources, including government. What makes these programs successful is a combination of personal commitment and a willingness to try to do something to bring about change in the lives of those who suffer.

It was incredibly easy to find these programs. I did some research in libraries, but even ordinary newspapers, magazines, religious periodicals, as well as radio and television, constantly seemed to be carrying stories about programs that work. Often I found myself reaching for my pad and pen during a public service advertisement about a new and creative solution to one of the problems I was studying. Before actually starting my writing I had the equivalent of a whole file drawer full of clippings, notes, pictures, and articles about good people working to alleviate misery around the world, in addition to dozens of files in my computer with information on these programs, those working in them, and the people being served.

Many times programs that start out very small and local become the basis for changes in law, for larger-scale developments, for whole movements. Mothers Against Drunk Driving (MADD) began with a few women who had lost children to drunk drivers and who eventually brought about a whole raising of consciousness in the country, a change of laws in many states, and a decrease in such deaths. Hospice started very small and has become a major movement that helps the dying and their families and caregivers. It is always dangerous to assume that because something is small and local its importance is small and limited. Small can be powerful, while remaining small. Small also can grow to be much bigger, without necessarily losing the values that characterized its small beginnings.

Many years ago E. F. Schumacher reminded us that "small is beautiful" and that it is often very successful!

ORIGINS OF THE STRATEGIES THAT WORK

At the end of this book, in addition to the usual list of references, a Source List is provided for those of you who want to do something similar to what you have read here. The list gives names and addresses of many successful programs based on the strategies that work. Some are described in the text of the book, others are only in the Source List. This list contains only a small sample of the hundreds of programs that are successful, but the sample gives a sense of the great diversity and creativity that is at work in our country and our world. It includes programs from the Two-Thirds World outside of the United States, and also from the Two-Thirds World which is within the United States.

Many of the strategies used in the United States had their origins in Africa or Asia. Reading a report from Inmed last year about a program in Washington, D.C., I found myself musing, "Ah, yes, that is like the village health workers and the traditional birth attendants in Ghana." When China, many years ago, began the training of the "barefoot doctors," health professionals in America and Europe were horrified. In fact, that program and many like it are not only successful in China, and Africa, and Asia—they are successful in America and Europe as well when given a chance.

Most of the Two-Thirds World countries were colonies until the 1950s and 1960s. As these new countries began to organize education, health, and social services, they had two things working in their favor. First, they did not have the money or the time to permit these to be developed by the private sector in the usual competitive modes of the First World. Second, they had the advantage of people with excellent minds who had studied the systems in the First World and had seen that they would help the few, but not the many. They were free to use their creativity and to innovate in ways that the First World often is not.

This is not to glamorize or idealize these struggling new countries. They also made mistakes, and not all that they tried worked out. However, as a foundation vice president said to me once when I was directing a series of pilot projects in community-based primary healthcare, we can learn as much from what doesn't work as from what does.

CHAPTER 6

Poverty as a Dead End

"There will always be poor people in the land...
I command you to be openhanded
toward the poor and needy."
(Deuteronomy 15:11)

F requently we hear people say somewhat complacently that we will always have the poor with us. This is a misuse and a misunderstanding of the words of Jesus to Judas when he complained about the woman who washed Jesus' feet with expensive nard. We interpret Jesus' statement to mean there is nothing to be done about poverty. We use it as a way to excuse ourselves from trying to change things. Jesus was telling Judas, and all of us since, that there will be people who are poor, who need to be assisted, and that it is our task to reach out to them with the same loving attention that Mary gave to Jesus as she washed his feet with that sweet smelling nard. How often do we actually treat the poor as Mary treated Jesus, with love, with personal attention that extends even to washing feet, using not the cheap soap from the supermarket, but the very expensive special soap?

THE PROBLEM OF POVERTY TODAY

Today there is a very dangerous trend. Although it has occurred in the past, it is no less tragic for not being new. Rather than a reaching out with compassion to the poor, what we see today is a blaming of the poor and, even more, a demonizing of them. We hear good people, including the leaders of government and industry, denigrating the poor as lazy, cheats, promiscuous, criminal...and characterizing them with other qualities that we despise. There is a growing movement of scapegoating the poor which is mean-spirited and based on faulty information.

Jim Wallis in *Sojourners* magazine often points out the tendency in Congress to focus attention on a number of government entitlements that help the poor. Such programs make up a much smaller part of the budget than many other government expenditures. More costly, indeed, are a whole range of middle-class and corporate subsidies which go unchallenged. Thus, the poor are not only deprived of help, but are also blamed for the economic problems of the country at large. While the current welfare system can be seen to be faulty, it is the poor themselves, because they are perceived as being relatively powerless, who are attacked.

The myths that form the basis for attacking the poor parallel other American myths about the self-made person, the rugged individualist who goes out and conquers all without depending on others. Robert Reich points to one of the recurring myths, that of the "triumphant individual." This is the person who works hard, takes risks, and eventually wins all. Implied in the myth of the self-made man or woman is the idea that this person did it *all alone* and unassisted, and second, that anyone who wishes to do so can do the same. Unexamined, it is in some ways a great myth. As an encouragement to people to work hard, to take risks, to strive, it has some value. However, like most myths, especially racial and ethnic ones, it leaves out important parts of the reality. As someone said to me once, "It's fine to pull yourself up by your bootstraps...assuming you have boots!"

This is part of the problem with the myth of self-sufficiency. When we read behind the lines of the stories of the superachievers we find hidden helps that are provided by others—family, friends, churches, even by the victims of the successful ones. The robber barons of the nineteenth century were considered self-made men, but they made themselves rich on the backs of poor immigrants. They also achieved success with a great deal of help from people like themselves, and from the government. Corporate welfare was not born in the latter part of the twentieth century!

The other problem with the myth is that we often exalt people of very questionable ethics, those who use a variety of nefarious methods to achieve their goals. Once, as a child, I was talking to my grandfather about the wonderful gifts of public libraries that Andrew Carnegie had made. My grandfather, while agreeing these were great gifts, remarked that they were made possible by the unfair labor practices of the Carnegie steel industry. He had been a union organizer in the years when the workers were trying to get a fair shake from the industry. In a sense, what he was saying was that the gift of the Carnegie libraries was less from Andrew Carnegie, and more from the workers who labored for low wages. It was *their* sacrifices, not self-chosen, which provided the funds for the libraries. As a daughter of the working class I found myself going into the public library with a new sense of pride and ownership, looking on it as something donated, not just by Carnegie, but by people like my grandfather.

In our own day, Jim Hug points out the reigning wisdom of the government conservatives which sees the present "problem" as a spiritual and moral one, in which the poor are trapped in a "culture of poverty," a culture of dependency on government programs. Poverty will never be overcome, the argument goes, until the poor themselves assume responsibility for their own lives. He asks if the real spiritual and moral problem is rather in the failure of government in its responsibilities to all the people.

CAUSES OF POVERTY TODAY

Poverty is not a new reality. Throughout history there have been cycles of great poverty, and others when things have been better for the majority. For many people of my generation, the Depression of the 1930s was a reality that was overcome by a war, which put most people to work and built large factories, and by the post-war reconstruction of Europe and large parts of Asia. Americans tend to speak with pride of what we did for reconstructing other countries, even those of our "enemies." What we tend to overlook is that the reconstruction of large parts of the world after World War II was a major factor in the American economic revival of the 1950s and 1960s. It was not unalloyed altruism that moved us. The situation provided a great economic opportunity for American industry, and therefore for the working class. As a nation we pride ourselves on not having been a colonial power, but for much of this century we have been a major economic colonizing power.

Now things are changing drastically. The countries we helped to rebuild have become economic powers themselves. From being the largest creditor nation we have become the largest debtor nation. Capitalism, like socialism, has failed in some very significant ways. This could lead us into blaming the new powers like Japan and Korea, especially those which have contributed to our trade imbalance. However, that is not the only source of our problems. A more important source is the economic system which we have developed, praised, and protected. The system of capitalism itself has become the enemy.

According to Willis Harman, the basic premise upon which so much of the world now functions is itself the problem. That premise holds that the economic system is the key, the paramount institution which should direct all social decisions. In a capitalistic system, decisions are best made by market mechanisms; if all act in self-interest, the resulting social decisions will serve the good of the whole. This is the theory. It doesn't work in practice because the system is based on the fallacy of unlimited growth.

There have been many calls for a new economic order, starting many years ago with the United Nations and fostered constantly by religious leaders including Pope John Paul II in his 1988 encyclical *Sollicitudo rei socialis*. When the Soviet Union and its satellites turned away from Communism, there was great rejoicing around the world. Now, however, in many of these countries where the people have, as expected, been politically empowered, the importation of the failed capitalism of the West has led to massive economic problems such as increased poverty, hunger, and homelessness. Those who had power under Communism still have power, but now they are the leaders of the emerging capitalism, and poverty is spreading among the working people.

In the United States, the almost unfettered sway of capitalism is creating more poverty as well. What has happened over the last twenty years that has taken us from relative prosperity for many to increased poverty for an increasingly larger portion of our people? Why have working-class people moved down the economic ladder during these years? There are many causes, just a few of which I want to highlight here.

One of the significant economic decisions made by many American industries has been to move factories and manufacturing first from the northeast to the south of the country, and then out of the country to places like Korea, the Philippines, and Mexico. The same reasons were behind each of the moves. The great mills of New England gradually closed as companies moved their plants south to get them into areas where there were few if any unions, where salaries and benefits to workers could be cut drastically, and where it was hoped that the unions would not follow. Anyone who saw the film *Norma Rae* knows what happened next. The unions went south! When the companies faced increasing demands for living wages, health benefits, and even simple protection from injury and death, they again moved. This time they moved to other countries where government regulations were fewer or non-existent, and where wages were minuscule in comparison with those in the United States. The maquilladoras of the Mexican border towns typify where American jobs went and the incredible injustices that went with them. Women working long hours for pitiful wages in these factories have replaced the union workers of the United States. It is a two-edged sword of injustice. And the reason for the injustice is the "bottom line" of profits.

The U.S. government has been a co-conspirator in this action. While making public statements about how the poor need to work rather than depend on welfare, it has given large tax breaks to the very corporations which have moved their operations to other countries, leaving many Americans unemployed. At the same time, those corporations were reaping large profits, paying CEOs incredibly large salaries, and reinvesting their profits not in their workers or in their plants, but in the stock market... money making money.

Chuck Collins, writing for *Network*, offers some soul-searing statistics about what has happened to people as a result of the economic decisions made by major corporations:

> *Income.* The 1 percent who are the wealthiest had increases of 110 percent in their incomes in the last fifteen years, while the bottom 60 percent of the population had their incomes stagnate or decline.
>
> *Wages.* The gap between the highest paid CEOs and their average workers has grown from 34-to-1 in the mid-1970s to over 179-to-1 today... Disney pays its CEO over 10,000 times more than the lowest paid workers.
>
> *Wealth.* The portion of wealth owned by the richest 1 percent of the population increased from 19 percent in 1976 to over 40 percent in 1996. This top 1 percent has more than the bottom 92 percent of the population.
>
> We are beginning to look like some of the developing nations of the world that we used to pity because such a small part of the population controlled so much of the wealth. The United States is at that same point now.

It is also important to realize that there have been significant changes in the taxes imposed by the government. During tax "reforms" of the 1980s, the tax rate on the nation's wealthiest was cut from 68 to 28 percent. In the last half century, corporations' federal tax revenue declined from 33 percent in the 1940s to less than 10 percent today. Individuals' share of the tax burden has increased from 43 to 76 percent. A great deal of so-called tax reform has in fact been a transfer of the tax burden from the wealthy to lower- and middle-class taxpayers. Tax code loopholes and subsidies are primarily designed for wealthy corporations and individuals, not for ordinary taxpayers.

A 1996 study, done by the Citizens for Tax Justice, shows that the poor and middle-class people in the United States pay a higher percentage of their income in state and local taxes than do the rich. According to the study: the richest 1 percent of the non-elderly married pay on average 7.9 percent of their income in these taxes, but the poorest 20 percent pay 12.5 percent. In some states, the proportion paid by poor people is four times that paid by the wealthy.

The government has helped many large corporations with subsidies, a form of corporate welfare. These come in many modes and are doled out to many industries: the tobacco industry (while Health and Human Services is trying to convince people of the dangers of smoking); large-scale agribusiness (in order to keep food prices up); the pharmaceutical industry (which gets government subsidies for research and development and then charges high prices to consumers to "get back the costs of research and development"). Other subsidies include oil and gas depletion allowances and low fees for grazing rights on national land to large-scale cattle growers. While receiving subsidies, many of these same industries are downsizing, moving their production off shore, and adding to the number of people below the poverty level, all the while speaking out against the lazy poor who don't want to work.

As we look at government and industry actions that create new pools of people in poverty, and recognize how many full-time workers still live on the edge of survival, it becomes even harder to accept the decisions which would remove the safety net from those who have little else. The 1996 welfare reform legislation passed by Congress, while praised as a step in the right direction by its sponsors, could well lead to a new surge of problems for the poor. Clearly, it will be potentially devastating for children.

In its annual report on hunger in 1996, Bread for the World identified two places in the world which have had dramatic increases in hunger: Africa and the United States. In Africa the increase in hunger over the previous three years ranged from 38 percent to 43 percent of the continent's population. In the United States hunger rose 50 percent between 1985 and 1995, from 20 million to 30 million, with 12 million being children under the age of 18. The movement toward block grants to states and responsibility for programs at the state level ignores the reason why so many programs had been originally shifted to the federal level. The vast discrepancies between services to the poor in the different states led to a call for federal intervention and equalization. Within weeks of the signing of the welfare "reform" bill, one state announced the removal of a large number of disabled children from support because they were not sufficiently disabled! (CNN news broadcast, Nov. 28, 1996, Thanksgiving day!)

It is not enough to talk about people getting jobs. We need to look at the systems in place which *in fact* eliminate the possibilities for jobs. The situation will not change just because we tell people that they must get work after two years on welfare. If there are no jobs, or no training possibilities, we will simply transfer the problems.

There is something deeply immoral (perhaps calling for divine retribution) about a society in which a small sliver of the population lives in excessive wealth and comfort while so many others are hungry or poor. Of the terrible discrepancies, one of the most incredible is in the area of CEO salaries. Chuck Collins gives a telling example. "The head of one leading healthcare company made $127 million in 1992. That's $60,000 an hour— or $16 a second. Along with excessive CEO compensation comes a widening wage gap. That same CEO's salary could pay wages for 3,000 nurses in the firm or 9,000 entry-level workers."

Many of the poor feel a growing sense of despair. There are those who want to work but have given up after years of trying to find jobs. Others have been "downsized" out of several jobs, one after another. Still others simply can't get any work at all. In my neighborhood we have teenagers who during the school year are in high school, but in the summer end up "hanging out." The tragedy is that they want to work, but have few opportunities. Sometimes there just are no jobs available, or they lack the simple skills they need. In a few cases they are racially discriminated against in strange new ways. Some African-American and Hispanic teens are being refused work by Asians who own many of the businesses in the area and primarily give jobs to relatives.

Women who are on welfare, on AFDC, look at minimum wage jobs with no health benefits and know they cannot *afford* to work if it means their children will have no health coverage. Worse than the poverty itself is the despair, the loss of hope, the sense of being caught in an impossible situation, in a no-win bind. And, finally, from all sides they hear themselves being blamed, called "welfare cheats," and accused of laziness.

Then there are the elderly in our midst. Through changes in healthcare and nutrition we have increased life expectancy in our country. Social Security and Medicare were devised to ensure that elderly people would have sufficient funds to sustain life. For the majority of the elderly these systems work, though concern about the viability of Social Security and threatened cutbacks on Medicare can create fear even among those who are fairly well off. For others, however, the systems don't work, so there are still many poor elderly in our country. These include widows living on a portion of their husbands' benefits, and people who worked their whole lives but in low-paying positions that now provide only minimum benefits from Social Security. They also include some of the elderly mentally ill who end up on the streets or in homeless shelters. Finally, they include those who for many reasons find themselves in their last years either without close relatives or ignored by families. Most of these people thought life would be safe after retirement. The poor who are elderly and abandoned are perhaps one of the saddest sights in soup kitchens and shelters.

As a people who consider ourselves to be religious and righteous, we need to remember some of the basics of our Judeo-Christian tradition. God speaking to Isaiah reminds us: "For the ruthless shall come to naught and the scoffer cease, and all who watch to do evil shall be cut off, who by a word make the innocent out to be offenders, and lay snares for those who would defend them, and with empty pleas turn aside those who are in the right"(Is 29:20-21).

STRATEGIES THAT DO NOT WORK

Current Welfare Programs

Among politicians, particularly the conservative groups that have benefited so much from the current economic philosophy and the systems flowing from it, the desire to balance the budget and to protect "our children" has overshadowed everything else. These politicians can unashamedly tout inhuman strategies that eliminate poverty, strategies that they know do not work.

One strategy that clearly does not work, and even its supposed beneficiaries will say the same, is the welfare system as it is. It does not work for a number of reasons. Primarily it has failed because it breaks up families, or militates against intact families. There are regulations which cut off funds to women and children if the father is in the home. The assumption, of course, is that if the father is there, he should be supporting the family. The possibility that he may be among the chronically unemployed is not considered.

Another problem with the current system and its suggested replacements, such as Workfare, or Welfare 2 in Wisconsin, is that the amount of money received by the families is only enough to keep them from starvation and homelessness. There is not enough to allow for further education for the parents or for the children. A tragic case several years ago was that of a teenage girl who had worked after school to be able to go to college. The family lost its welfare benefits, and the girl lost the money she had earned, as well the opportunity to better herself by education. It is the inexorable cycle of dead-ending people that makes the current system so sinful.

There is a need for welfare reform. The current suggestions, however, are more truly welfare dismantlement, based on the vague notion that somehow, within two to five years, those now in the system will be able to work and live on what they earn. Questions relating to the long-standing unemployment levels at more than 5 percent, the paucity of benefits in so many entry-level jobs available to the very poor, and the insufficiency of the often fought over minimum wage itself, are never answered.

While many people would agree on the importance of having a more effective, value-centered approach, what is actually happening is that the safety net is being dismantled, while the responsibility for welfare assistance is being relegated to the states, with no uniform system of accountability.

The Criminalization of Poverty

Another strategy that does not work is the criminalization of the poor. In some cases it is a matter of charging the poor with crimes because of what their poverty forces them to do. There are stories of women leaving small children alone in houses or apartments—or even in cars—while they work. The resulting outrage, even if nothing bad happens, ignores the fact that at the pay these women receive they cannot afford to provide even the simplest levels of child care. My generation grew up in extended families; grandparents, aunts, uncles, and cousins could be called upon to help out with the children while parents had to work. I remember my mother caring for two cousins while their parents were starting a small business. I have no idea if there was any money exchanged. When there were family needs, there always seemed to be relatives around who could be counted on. For many people today the extended family simply does not exist.

Another form of criminalizing is what happens with so many homeless who are hounded through our streets because of the discomfort they cause the rest of us. An upscale restaurant in one city complained to the police because a homeless man was sitting on a vent, for warmth, in view of the patrons who were dining on expensive meals in the restaurant. The sight of him made those diners uncomfortable, though obviously not uncomfortable enough to help him.

There are homeless parents who are charged with not having their children in school, when they cannot get them into schools because they have no address. Nor can they apply for public assistance for the same reason. All these examples relate to looking at poverty as being the fault of those who are poor. If there is a crime, it is not in being poor, but in being hardened and blind to the desperate situations of many poor people.

Low-paying Jobs

Among the cruelest of the strategies that do not work are those that seem like they should work, but do not, and so are illusory solutions. Chief among these is the suggestion that people should go to work for the minimum wage or less, with no benefits, not even essential ones like health insurance. While such jobs may be acceptable for teenagers working after school, or possibly as starter jobs for single persons entering the work world, they make no sense for adults with children to support. It is hard-hearted and callous to suggest that this kind of work is better than welfare for people with families. Too often the people we see speaking in favor of such jobs on the evening news are politicians with well-paying jobs, excellent health coverage for themselves and their families, and numerous perks which add to their basic income.

Recently, while talking to a friend who is a social worker, I heard about her expenses just to get to the job she held. Her basic transportation was $25.00 a week, on public transport. She told of packing lunches, because she could not afford to pay $5–10 each day to buy her lunch at downtown cafeterias or fast-food places. Since she was working in a social agency, she felt she could dress very simply in skirts and blouses. As we talked, she reinforced what I already knew, that a minimum wage job (which she did not have) could not begin to meet the needs of an adult with children to support.

The welfare mother who gives up AFDC—along with the health insurance that is included—to work for the minimum wage must pay for public transportation, clothes for work, lunches and, in addition, pay someone to take care of her children while she is at work. One does not need a degree in economics to know that this is not going to balance out. Even worse, since she will have no health insurance for herself or her children, she has to hope that no one becomes ill. If a child does become ill, she may have to risk losing her job by taking time off to take the child to a public health clinic, where she may spend the whole day in the waiting room before seeing a doctor.

Orphanages and Workhouses

A few years ago, one of our well-known politicians suggested that one of the solutions would be to reinstitute orphanages for the children of welfare parents. He is the same man who frequently talks about family values. It is hard to see how putting children in orphanages because their parents are poor is in any way a support of family life and values. He has suggested as well

that we reestablish the workhouses of the last century. Charles
Dickens documented for us just how ineffective the workhouses of nineteenth-century England actually were. They broke up
families, separated children and parents, and put people to
work in situations which would ensure that they never achieved
any kind of independence.

Doubling Jobs

What is often completely ignored is that not all families in need
are headed by unemployed people on welfare. There are many
families in which both parents work to support their children.
This is not a case of women working in order to get an extra
television set or pay for a trip to the seashore. This is a case of
both parents working so that the basics of housing, food, clothing, healthcare, and education are available for the family. In
my neighborhood, I see couples doing this. Often the parents
work two different shifts, one a day shift and the other an
evening or night shift, so that the children are never left at
home alone. This is admirable and I think a great lesson for
the children, but it is not what we mean when we talk of family
life and values. It is a strategy that works in terms of obtaining
sufficient income, but it does not necessarily work in terms of
providing the best care for children, and especially for
teenagers. Children who see how hard their parents have to
work, who cannot count on having someone there when they
need them, or who feel that they should not further burden
their parents, are more likely to become discouraged in school
and have problems in other areas.

STRATEGIES THAT WORK

Tax Incentives and Reform

One major source of the poverty that is strangling many people
is the injustice of the tax laws, which put an unfair burden on
middle- and lower-income people, and give huge breaks to the
wealthiest people. We hear a lot about budget balancing and
tax reform, specifically, the kind of tax reform that gives tax advantages to corporations and to the wealthy, on the assumption

that such breaks will create new jobs and thus indirectly help the poor. There is nothing in the current situation that in any way supports that assumption. In fact, jobs are being lost continuously as corporations move to other countries and as the new technologies lead to large-scale downsizing and job loss. In 1996 the Congressional Budget Office proposed *export aid* to General Electric and Westinghouse! The special exemptions that make it possible for individuals and companies to make large amounts of tax-free money in the stock market have more to do with making money than with the development of new jobs. "Trickle down" economics is a failed system that needs to be recognized for what it was, a means for justifying the growing divide between the "haves" and the "have nots."

Government, at federal, state, and local levels, could be giving special tax incentives to corporations that *create* new jobs, that provide training for employees downsized out of one job so they can continue working at a new job. In February 1996, Senator Bingaman of New Mexico presented a detailed plan to provide incentives for corporations to behave more responsibly toward their employees, the communities in which they exist, and the country as a whole. He proposed that businesses operating in the United States could qualify for status as a "Business Allied with America's Working Families" or an "A-Corp." A business so qualified would receive extremely favorable tax, regulatory, and government contract treatment. Requirements for qualification would include: contributions to a pension plan; an amount equal to 2 percent of payroll applied to employee training and education; payment of at least half of a healthcare plan; operating a profit sharing, gain sharing, or stock option plan in which at least 50 percent of employees participate; ensuring that the highest paid employee's compensation was no higher than 50 times that of the lowest paid full-time employee; ensuring that at least 50 percent of all new investment in research and development occur in the United States; maintaining above-average occupational safety and environmental compliance records. The purpose of the legislation is to encourage and reward those businesses which are willing to trade short-term profits for long-term investments in employees as a form of alliance with the working families of the country. The legislation has received a lukewarm reception and as yet the plan has not been introduced into Congress.

Mergers of corporations into larger mega-corporations are viewed by government in terms of anti-trust laws. Government needs to consider as well the effects of these mergers on the employees of the companies. It also needs to consider the effects on the communities in terms of loss of jobs or sometimes loss of access to certain services like banks and supermarkets. Either tax breaks for those companies which are socially responsible, or tax charges for those which are not, could make a significant difference in the lives of the individuals and communities impacted by corporate decisions.

Welfare-Workfare

It is important to create welfare reforms that can work. To simply eliminate welfare after a set amount of time may assuage the consciences of the legislators, but will not be of help to the poor. Moving people from welfare to work that is good, productive, and pays a *living wage*, as opposed to the minimum wage, is going to require much more creativity than is being exhibited by the present suggestions.

A number of years ago, one of my classmates in our doctoral program worked as an intern with the City of Philadelphia in an innovative program for welfare mothers, an experimental program that had great potential for breaking the cycle of poverty. The mothers continued receiving welfare funds while they were enrolled in training programs that guaranteed jobs at the end of the training. An important aspect of the program was the fact that the training was connected with companies which were looking for specific workers and were willing to hire the new trainees. Once the women started working, they were guaranteed enough welfare so that what they earned and their welfare funds combined amounted to more than they would have received simply on welfare. This made it possible for them to take entry-level jobs with some future, even though the jobs paid less than welfare. As they moved up in the jobs and in salary, the welfare benefits gradually decreased. This provided a true safety net for them and for their children while they worked their way out of the dependency.

Training Programs

One of the simplest solutions to poverty is the provision of training for jobs. However, the jobs have to actually exist and pay a living wage. There are a variety of programs around the country designed to provide basic and specific education and training to help people in poverty make a first step on the road out of welfare. In Baltimore, the Franciscan Center provides a variety of emergency services: clothing, financial assistance, groceries, and lunches for the very poor in the area. However, the center goes beyond that to provide programs in adult literacy and basic skills training that have led to jobs for many of their graduates. This is one example of a neighborhood program funded by donations from many sources and using space provided by a religious congregation of women which has a long history of reaching out to the poor.

While women are in job training programs, many of which are run by not-for-profit volunteer groups, a constant concern is what is happening to their children. Whether job training is done by city social services, church, or volunteer groups, programs offered should include training in child care. Thus, while some women are learning computer or data processing skills, other women could be learning what is needed to set up and run in-home licensed day care programs.

One of our neighbors, with three pre-school children and one in school, was unable to get work that would help her to support her children and still provide for their care while she was working. She looked into the requirements for becoming a day care provider. She obtained a license, and eventually was taking care of twelve children five days a week. Some went to the local school, so she had them before and after school and escorted them to and from the school. The pre-schoolers were with her all day. In this way she was able to provide for herself and her children, while filling a very large need for other area families with two working parents. She went on to get her high school diploma and hopes to take some community college courses so she can become a legal secretary.

Another area for training is that of entrepreneurial work. Too often we think of this kind of work as limited to the well-educated professional who wants to work independently. Although some forms of work require high levels of education, the small independent business is within the realm of possibility for many more people. Some cities have begun developing programs to help people set up their own small businesses, such as beauty shops in the home, home secretarial and computer services. The programs, which often use skills that the new entrepreneurs already have and add to them, include training in how to run a small business, how to charge and bill, and how to keep track of taxes. Our neighbor was proud to be able to say that she was paying taxes on her small in-home day care business!

Several years ago I heard Ann Stallard, then president of the YWCA, talk about a program the Y had undertaken in Chicago with people living in a housing project that had many families from Appalachia. The women, many of whom were on welfare, were poorly educated and had children at home. The people from the Y discovered that some of these women had learned the art of quilt making from their families. With a small grant to get started and to buy materials, a group of women began quilting, as their grandmothers had done for generations. They set up a small cooperative and, with some training in organizing and marketing, began selling their quilts. Other women in the housing project, uninterested in quilting, became the paid child care contingent for the quilters. Eventually, the co-op was so successful that the families no longer qualified for public housing, but by then they had a thriving small business which continues, even though they now live in other housing. The incredible part of this story, to me, was that all the skill was there, but what was needed was a catalyst to help the women to see that a hobby could become a business.

In Anthony, New Mexico, there is another cooperative for women, the Mujeres Unidas Cooperative. It was formed by women of the area who were looking for economic alternatives for themselves and their families. They started by taking part in the Women's Intercultural Center, a project initiated by the Sisters of Mercy to be a place "to support one another, to share our cultures, to learn to live our faith, to talk about our problems, and to learn practical things." The center, a bilingual place where "all women are welcome," offered workshops on carpentry, sewing, cooking, and language learning, as well as on such topics as self-esteem, nutrition, and health. The Mujeres Unidas Cooperative makes and markets futons, quillows (a pillow that becomes a quilt), cloth bags, and colorful vests. This is a self-help project of a group that also has dedicated itself to being environmentally conscious in its work.

Similar cooperatives could be developed in neighborhoods if some energy were given to exploring with people what they could do. A number of churches in poverty areas have set up food co-ops. In these, members pool their funds for food buying so that it can be bought wholesale or from food distribution centers. In addition to the money put in, which is a small amount regularly, the members also devote a certain number of hours each week to working in the co-op. One of the co-ops I studied was able after some time to hire several of the people in the neighborhood to do the buying at the food distribution center and to pick it up in a small truck. This community effort provided lower-cost food to everyone and several jobs to people in the area who had been unemployed.

Social Consciences in Corporations

In many cities there are corporations that have received large tax breaks from those cities to relocate there. It becomes important to ensure that those corporations do not get additional incentives that lead to a loss of jobs in the areas to which they have relocated, making the situation worse for the people who originally invited them. Those corporations need to be encouraged or perhaps even required to make some payback to the people of the community. A few corporations have done this on their own, whether for good public relations or out of a true sense of social responsibility. One national corporation, Fashion Bug (a part of Charming Shoppes, which has 1100 stores in forty-five states), has a CEO who is committed to community involvement at both the corporate level and in the local communities where the stores are located. In November 1996 the company's program "Keeping Kids Warm" distributed new winter coats to five hundred elementary school children in a poverty area in Philadelphia. The aim of this program is to provide coats to children around the country in areas where the need is greatest. In November 1997 the local stores announced a continuation of the program for another year.

In some places corporations "adopt" inner city schools, providing computers or other materials for them. Sometimes they offer work-study programs for high school students within their corporate structures. The employees of these companies are encouraged and assisted in becoming involved with the communities where they work through a variety of programs, such as tutoring school children, helping with adult literacy, coaching sports, and sponsoring local community job projects. Not only are people helped, but the companies themselves benefit. Their corporate image is enhanced, their employees are energized by the experience of reaching out, and eventually, the companies reap the benefits of better prepared entry-level employees from the community.

Another way that corporations can be of help to their own employees and to their communities is by providing day care programs within their plants. This can make life less stressful for their employees who may have difficulty finding affordable day care, and it can provide child care work for women in the community.

Banking for and with the Poor

Many poor neighborhoods find that banks are fleeing, cutting back on services, and showing great reluctance to make loans—even mortgages—in the area. This may make sense to the banks, but it creates serious problems for poor neighborhoods. Banks, like all corporations, have to develop a greater social conscience, especially in the communities where they are pursuing their business. Often banks appear to think with blinders on their brains. They act from a base of assumptions that are strongly focused against the poor.

All banks could learn from the experience of Mohammed Yunus, the founder of the Grameen Bank in Bangladesh. So often we hear that the things that can be done in the First World will not work in the Two-Thirds World. Here is a case where the Two-Thirds World has been successful in something that the First World often will not even consider. The Grameen

Bank has demonstrated with incredible success that the very poorest people can borrow money, start businesses, make a success of them and—to the joy of the bank—pay back the loans on time. It is best to hear the story in the words of Mohammed Yunus:

In Bangladesh we run a bank for the poor. We think of the poor differently. We think they are as capable and as enterprising as anybody else. Circumstances have just pushed them to the bottom of the heap. They work harder than anybody else. They have more skills than they get a chance to use. With a supportive environment, they can pull themselves out of the heap in no time. Back in 1976, we offered tiny loans to the poorest people in one village. People showed how good they were at using the money to earn income and pay the loans back. They were honest and hard working but that's not how conventional bankers choose to see the poor. To them, the poor belong to the class of the untouchables. Encouraged by our initial results, we expanded our work to two villages, ten villages, one district, and then five districts. At no point did we have any problem getting our money back. But all along, conventional bankers told us: "What you are seeing is not the real thing. The real thing is that the poor have no will to work, they have no ability. They will never return your money." For a while, we felt confused. What was real? What we heard about the poor, or what we experienced with the poor? We relied on our experience. We kept expanding. Today, Grameen Bank, the poor peoples' bank in Bangladesh, operates in 34,000 villages, exactly half the number of villages in Bangladesh. Grameen Bank currently lends money to 1.7 million borrowers, 94 percent of whom are women. The borrowers own the bank. We lend out over $30 million each month in loans averaging less than $100. The repayment rate is over 98 percent. Besides generating loans, we also give housing loans. A typical housing loan is $300. We have given more than 220,000 housing loans so far with a perfect repayment record. Studies done on Grameen tell us that the borrowers have improved their income, widened their asset base and moved steadily toward crossing the poverty line and toward a life of dignity and honor. Studies also tell us that in Grameen families the nutrition level is better than in non-Grameen families, child mortality is lower and adoption of family planning practices is higher. All studies confirm the visible empowerment of women. (Quoted in Donaher, 1994)

First-World banks need to pay attention to the experience of the Grameen Bank. Hardheadedness in business is not always assisted by hardheartedness. If this program can work in one of the poorest countries of the world, it can also work in one of the richest. What is needed is the commitment to try. A significant element in the success of the Grameen Bank's efforts was its conscious decision to begin by targeting *women*. By actually going out and convincing women that they could start their own small cottage businesses, and assuring them that the bank would lend them the money, the Grameen Bank took an unusual step for a Muslim business in a Muslim country. However, these men knew of the power and the strength of women who wanted to provide a better life for their children. A growing number of banks in the United States are following the lead of the Grameen Bank and are introducing micro-lending to their customers and potential customers.

The Report of the United Nations Expert Group on Women and Finance 1994 meeting, which was convened by Women's World Banking, documents many other ways in which financial institutions can help poor women move out of poverty. In Anthony, New Mexico, the home of the Women's Intercultural Center mentioned above, there is a new venture in banking as well. The Banco Internacional de la Mujer, the International Women's Bank, opened in 1994. It is based on a similar project, FEMAP, which has helped start twenty-eight community banks in Mexico. FEMAP trained nine women and set up an initial fund to get the bank in Anthony started. The bank provides small loans at very low interest to women who want to start their own businesses. The loans start at $100 and can gradually be increased as the borrowers demonstrate their ability to meet the low-interest payments and establish their businesses. One group of four women pooled their loans and started the first tortilla factory in Anthony. One of the partners in the effort is the University of Texas in El Paso which provides training in marketing and is researching the impact of community banking.

Over the past several decades a number of church and religious bodies have made deliberate decisions to move their money, investments, and business to banks that function with a social conscience. Most groups have had difficulty finding such banks. Often they have discovered them among minority-owned banks, and those owned or operated by women. In January 1996 Georgetown University announced that it was investing one million dollars in a newly developing bank, First Community Bank of D.C. This new bank has been designed to serve low- and moderate-income neighborhoods in the District of Columbia. It hopes to be able to work closely with local financial institutions to increase access and responsible use of credit, and with community organizations to produce affordable housing and encourage entrepreneurship. Its efforts will include making commercial, real-estate, and consumer loans available in an area of the city which has lacked all of these services.

Many small businesses do not require large capital, but they find that banks are not interested in the small loans. Mohammed Yunus started with extremely small loans and expanded to very large-scale business for the bank and for the communities in which it exists. The First Community Bank of D.C. may experience the same kind of success in Washington.

The First African Methodist Episcopal Church of Los Angeles is an example of a church that has moved directly into the financial field. It gives low-interest loans to minority business people. While not every local church can match this effort, it is possible for a church to set up a form of credit union among its members to help those who cannot get loans from ordinary banks. Government can also help through legislation that rewards banks for social awareness and programs that help the poor. An example is HR3464, 1995, Community Development Banking which authorizes $382 million to community development financial institutions for loans, grants, deposits, and equity investments for underserved and poor areas.

Everyone can help by simply going into their local bank, the one in which they do business, and asking about the bank's policies regarding loans to small businesses, loans to poor people who want to get started, and mortgage programs that assist the poor rather than deterring them from owning their own homes. Many religious congregations and churches have made the placement of their funds in banks contingent on the social conscience and actual programs of those banks. This is using the power of a bank customer to help others.

Unified efforts by groups can have an impact on local situations. Thus, a parish can have an impact on a bank if it discusses the relationship between its choice of bank and the social policies of that bank. If all the parishes in an area or a whole diocese were to make a stand regarding banking and social action, the effect on the banks of the area would undoubtedly be greater.

Collaborative Efforts

Collaboration is especially important for those organizations that work with the poor, because a coordinated effort is essential. While each group may have its own special interest, its own areas of competency, and its own programs, much greater things can be accomplished if all the groups work together. Within a state, if the various religious organizations that work with and for the poor were to collaborate and coordinate their strategies, their impact on state governments would be greater. In Ohio, for example, there has been discussion of reorganizing the networks of church social services, perhaps into one statewide service, in order to facilitate access to the "block grants" currently on the federal plan for the states. Such networking would assist church groups in obtaining necessary funds. It would reduce, as well, the possibility of having dioceses or different churches competing for the same funds. Churches must speak out for those who have no voice. They are most effective when they are heard *as one*, even while speaking from different traditions.

Within cities, community action groups need to work together with those in nearby communities to increase their power to help themselves and one another. As a unified group they have a much greater impact on government and on businesses and industries in their geographic areas. One such group, the Olney Community Council in Philadelphia, working with other neighborhood organizations, recently blocked the closing of the only neighborhood supermarket until the company agreed to sell the property only to another supermarket. It was the combined effort of several groups that made this possible. A new supermarket is now using the space vacated by the original one.

Individuals often feel at a loss to know how to impact government. They need to be aware that not all political action groups are self-serving. Many have been formed, and more are needed, to commit themselves to the poor. Powerful Voices, a group of community action groups, collaborates in helping low-income people get access to the political realm for legislation to help them. Network is another powerful lobbying group. Founded by religious women committed to a more just society, it lobbies for and keeps its members informed on the movement of legislation through Congress. Its publication, *Network Connection,* regularly lists what various senators and representatives are voting for and against. This is very helpful for individuals and groups who want to write, phone, or talk face-to-face with the people they have placed in office. People need to work together to make their representatives aware that *they* are aware of what is happening for and against the poor in the halls of Congress.

Creation of Community Jobs

One of the things which has to happen, and can be successfully accomplished, is the development of new jobs in neighborhoods and communities all over America that have been devastated by the closure of plants, factories, and mills. In many poor areas, when major plants close other businesses move out: grocery stores, clothing stores, small restaurants. Merchants sometimes close because of violence and robberies. Often banks are unwilling to give loans for new businesses in the area.

The normal patterns of life disappear. This is one of the saddest of experiences for the people.

A coalition of neighborhood community groups can be very effective. In collaboration with the police, it can begin to organize and capture back the neighborhood for the people themselves. What is needed is a commitment of the people, the local government, the police, and the lending institutions. Churches can be a strong force for support and encouragement. While it is commonplace to find neighborhoods organizing for street cleanups and anti-crime safety, it is just as important for the groups to look at how they can increase the viability of small businesses in the area. Organizations of neighborhoods can lobby city government to foster new businesses and industries in those areas which have lost the old ones, and where buildings which are slowly decaying are still salvageable.

With increased numbers of women working today there is a need for safe and affordable child care. Childspace is one response to this need. While helping working parents by caring for their children, it offers training and jobs to low-income people. This worker-owned cooperative has two centers in which it serves 235 children and employs 35 staff members, most of whom have come out of the low-income bracket. The workers receive a better compensation program than the industry standard, are trained to function professionally, and develop a sense of ownership and therefore responsibility. Childspace serves as a model for other programs.

A very interesting example of the fostering of new business and a better life for people comes from the Two-Thirds World. It is the story of Curitiba, Brazil, and is told here by Bernard A. Lietaer. He writes:

> When Jaime Lerner became mayor of the medium-sized Brazilian town of Curitiba in 1973, he had a tricky garbage collection problem. The majority of the 500,000 people of Curitiba lived in shanty towns (*favelas*), which had been built so haphazardly that even the garbage trucks could not get into them. The accumulation of garbage attracted rodents, which in turn spread diseases at alarming rates. The classical solution

would have been a welfare program to try to clean up the mess, but Lerner did not have that option because there were too few rich people in Curitiba, and the necessary funds were not available. The mayor was forced to invent another way. His solution was to pay public transport tokens to people for their garbage, under the condition that they presort and deposit it in recycling bins around the *favelas*. For organic waste, which was composted for use by farmers as fertilizer, people received chits that could be exchanged for food. The program worked spectacularly. The *favelas* were clean-picked by the kids, who quickly learned to distinguish between the different types of recyclable products. People could leave the *favelas* by public transport and travel to the center of town where the jobs were. The additional buses and gasoline were paid for with the proceeds from the sale of the presorted garbage to the glass, paper, and metal manufacturing companies. Even "normal" money was saved because fewer trucks and less gasoline were required to pick up the presorted garbage. And all this does not even include the savings due to reduced disease and a more efficient labor market. Today, Curitiba is clean, prosperous, and self-sufficient, and the only Brazilian city I know to refuse money from the state. It has a state-of-the-art public transportation system and a popular mayor who has been repeatedly reelected. Perhaps most significant, a strong sense of community and pride has arisen in a place where none was visible before.

In another example from Brazil, there is the story of the Base Christian Community in Alagoinhas, Brazil. In this very poor town, the people have organized themselves and elected community leaders. They have begun to build a community center, to construct tanks to collect rainwater, to grow vegetable gardens, and to organize cooperatives for small farmers. With the help of funds from the Brazilian government, the Medical Mission Sisters have trained health promoters for the village.

Both of these examples from Brazil show how, with limited funds but with cooperation among community action groups and the local government, particular problems can be addressed, life can be made better by the people themselves, and jobs can be created.

Peter Mann and Jennifer Urff in an article in *Network Connection* address the great scarcity of jobs in America.

> It is certainly true that jobs are scarce. More than 17 million Americans who want to work full time either don't have jobs or can only find part-time positions; another 18 million work year-round, full time, but still earn less than the poverty level of a family of four. Even in areas of relatively low unemployment, the number of job seekers far exceeds the number of available full-time jobs, especially for job seekers with no post-high school training or in poor areas.

However, they are not daunted by the statistics, calling attention rather to the immense number of things that need to be done in most poor areas and the possibility of combining those needs with the desire for work.

> ...the reality is that there is no end of work to be done. Our ability to create jobs is limited only by our imagination and our willingness to make work a priority for investment. Unmet social needs in our communities abound. We need teachers for our public schools, preventive healthcare, affordable housing, environmental cleanup and safer neighborhoods.

What they are calling attention to is the basic reality that many of the things that need to be done in neighborhoods are being done by volunteers but could become the basis for creating jobs. There are endless possibilities for entrepreneurial efforts, for a neighborhood-based job corps where neighbors pay one another for what needs to be done, thus providing neighborhood work for local people with skills in areas such as home repair or child care.

Local government could assist with the creation of public-sector jobs *that need to be done* combined with an investment in community-based work that meets real needs. Often we hear negative reactions to public-sector jobs for poor people, though the reaction is not so negative to other public-sector jobs, such as jobs done by social workers, police, fire fighters, teachers, and politicians. If the community needs the work done, then it would help to give these jobs to people who want to work and can do what is needed. After the great snow storm of January 1996 when Philadelphia had 31 inches of snow within twenty-four hours, the city managed to clear only the major roads and a few access roads. Many groups of neighbors chipped in to pay local residents with snow plows to clear the smaller streets so that all could get to work. That is an example of real community work being done by people in the community and benefiting everyone. Blizzards do not happen every year, but many community needs do recur regularly, and could form a basis for work.

In most cities there are many jobs which are not done because the work force is simply too small...and at the same time there are people looking for work. We need a new burst of creativity to bring together the people who need work with the jobs that the community needs done. Time Dollars is a program in St. Louis, Missouri, where people do work that is needed by their neighbors, and then get "time dollars" which can be traded in for money, food, or other services.

Another interesting approach is a program called Connections in Pasco County, Florida. Joan Foley, a Medical Mission Sister working in the St. Petersburg Free Clinic, began to hear of the needs in Pasco County, thirty miles north of where she lived and worked. In Pasco County there were few jobs (though the situation has improved) but the main difficulty for poor people was in assessing their skills, learning how to explain their skills to potential employers, and having the confidence to believe they could improve their situation. The program Joan Foley started is basically a job development program that reaches out to the poor to help them help themselves economically. It brings together businesses that need employees with the unemployed. Connections now maintains contact with employers in the county, counsels and directs the unemployed to potential jobs, and interrelates with other social agencies, programs, and churches. The first support for the work came from two parishes willing to share initial costs, plus some seed money from the Medical Mission Sisters Development Fund.

In Dorchester, Massachusetts, Independent Fabrication Inc. is an employee-owned manufacturer of high-performance bicycle frames used by mountain bikers. Committed to hiring and training low-income workers, the company anticipates having twenty full-time jobs by its fifth year of operation. It has won high praise from specialized biking magazines for its quality work. Initial funding came through a grant from the Campaign for Human Development, which has as one of its criteria for funding the empowerment of people. And, in this small company, people have been empowered. Since every worker is also an owner, every worker experiences both responsibility and pride, things that some of these people have never known before.

What is often lost in the political rhetoric is the basic fact that people would rather earn their money than take handouts. The loss of human dignity, the resulting low self-esteem, and the despair of long-term welfare families are the causes rather than the result of people giving up. People who move through training programs into jobs constantly demonstrate their joy at becoming independent of the welfare system. The angriest of the poor are often those who have experienced no other way of life and who know they are looked down on by the rest of society. What they see on television and hear in the speeches of some politicians endlessly reminds them of this. Despair is a dreadful reality, but it does not have to be if people are determined to help one another forward.

CHAPTER 7

Homelessness

*"Jesus replied, 'Foxes have holes and birds of the air have nests,
but I, myself have nowhere to lay my head.'"*
(Matthew 8:20)

If there is a scandalous situation in the United States today, one for which the richest nation in the world might well hang its head, it is the plight of the homeless. Over four million people were homeless in 1995.

This is not a new problem. However, the size of the current problem, and the apparent indifference—even callousness— of many people is hard to comprehend. Since those who have no homes are limited in their access to bathing and laundry facilities, they often seem dirty and smelly. Still, the pathetic picture of an old woman pushing a supermarket cart piled with her pitiful belongings through the streets of our large and small cities should move us to compassion. Too often it moves us to anger or to abhorrence and avoidance.

It is well known that the actual number of homeless is greater than the published figures. Many people who have lost their own homes double up with other family members or friends, and thus are not counted as "homeless." While it's important that family members reach out to one another, this type of assistance can often lead to other problems because of crowding, strains on the family's budget, and the despair created by those dependent people.

THE CAUSES OF HOMELESSNESS TODAY

Economic System

Most of the major causes of homelessness in this country are the same as those of poverty. One of the major causes is the current economic system that has enlarged the number of unemployed, and sometimes unemployable, adults. What can be most devastating is the reality that when people lose jobs, they can also lose homes because of their inability to keep up mortgage payments. For many men, the shame and horror of going through eviction and seeing their wives and children living in cars and trucks is so overwhelming that they end up abandoning their families. Initially, the idea is that the man will go and find work somewhere else, and then send for his family. How do you send for a family that is living on the streets with no address? In a best case scenario, the family is reunited after some time and life begins again. In a worst case scenario, the family is split up, with women and children in one overnight shelter and the men in another or completely gone from the scene.

Some people are homeless as a result of the hope-filled migration from rural to urban areas following the loss of a farm. The advent of large scale agri-business has been devastating for small family farms. There is no way that the small farmer can compete with the mega-businesses that have taken over most of the farm land. The city is traditionally seen as the mecca for the poor, the place where jobs are available and people can make a better life for themselves.

I was in New Delhi, India, in 1979. One night we went to see the light and sound show at the Red Fort. As we came out into the streets around the fort and waited for a city bus to get us back to our hostel, I saw hundreds of people, including women and children, curled up on sidewalks sleeping. One of the Indian sisters with me explained that these people had come from villages, hoping to find a better life in the city. What they found instead was even greater destitution. As she spoke, I became aware of her assumption that this would happen in her country, but not in mine. With considerable shame, I had to tell her the same kind of thing could be seen in my country.

The difference is that it is usually warm in New Delhi, while in Philadelphia and New York and Boston, and many other American cities, the winters are very cold. As so often happens when I am in the Two-Thirds World, people assume that I am seeing something that I would never see in the rich First World.

Another type of migration that occurs is from one part of the country to another when jobs have been lost due to downsizing or moving of companies, factories, and mills to another area. Just the thought that there might be jobs elsewhere can lead to an uprooting of the whole family as the parents search for work.

Mental Health Problems

Although some of the causes of homelessness today are the same as those in the 1930s, there are additional causes that have been created by other changes. The mental health legislation of thirty years ago was aimed at putting an end to the warehousing of the mentally ill. The dream (and as a predoctoral student in psychology at the time I was as excited as anyone about it) was that these people would be cared for in more humane group homes and treated through community mental health centers, and that families would be assisted in this great effort. No one who saw the inside of the worst of those mental hospitals would want a return to that failed system. However, what was supposed to replace it also failed, because the funds needed to make the dream a reality fell far short of what was required.

The vast majority of the homeless are not mentally ill. However, some of the homeless are mentally disadvantaged. These are people with serious lifelong disabilities as well as victims of depression, schizophrenia, and the character disorders that often stretch families beyond what they can manage. Estimates put the number of these people at no more than 10 to 15 percent of the homeless. Most have not *come* to homelessness because of mental disabilities, but many homeless people are undoubtedly stressed mentally by the horror of their situation.

Since the impression initially was that most homeless were mentally ill, there was a sense of discomfort as the "bag ladies" began showing up in shopping areas. Most gravitated toward the centers of cities, simply because there were so many chances for handouts as well as access to public and semi-public facilities. One of the first of the alternative programs in Philadelphia to aid the homeless was started by a group of religious sisters who went out every night to the railroad stations, the stops on the rapid transit systems, and other public places to give out sandwiches and coffee to the homeless. Many of the first people reached by the sisters were, in fact, mentally ill homeless women. The sisters were arrested several times before the public became as outraged over this as they were becoming at the sight of the homeless on their streets. The sisters' program has grown to include men, women, and children, and reaches well beyond the original mentally incapacitated homeless.

One young boy named Trevor made national news when he asked his parents to take him downtown so he could give his blankets to some of the homeless people. He became a hero. The actions of the sisters, and of a young suburban boy, began to change people's ideas about who the homeless were and how they had come to be homeless. These and other experiences began a movement toward reaching out to help them.

Family Breakups

A major source of homelessness among women and children is the breakup of families for reasons other than economic ones. The laws of the land are very hard to enforce when the husband/father leaves the city and even the state and stops the child support payments agreed upon at the time of a divorce. Not all of these men are low-income workers. There is a startlingly high number of middle-class homeless women and children whose situation has been created by the flight of the father after a divorce. Women who married young, thinking that they would be cared for, suddenly find themselves with children, no home, and few if any skills to get work. Even if they could work, it is almost impossible for these women to find jobs. Because they are homeless, they have no address, no phone, and no place for their children.

Stephanie Golden, who worked for several years as a volunteer in a program called the Dwelling Place, points to the loss of relationships as one of the key factors for many homeless women. She writes about the devastating effects of the loss of the primary relationship within a marriage. Most of the women she met and interviewed were of a generation that had been socialized to work in the home and be dependent on their husbands for income and other major personal supports. When these marriages broke up, the loss of the relationship was as devastating as the economic problems.

Educational Deficits

Another source of homelessness is chronic unemployment. Many of the homeless are people who simply do not have the basic skills for any kind of long-term remunerative employment. The illiteracy rate in America is almost as high as that in some Two-Thirds World countries. Even very simple work requires basic literacy. The change in the economic base of the United States, with the movement of mills and factories out of the country, has reduced drastically the kinds of jobs that can be held with very little education. As I watch grade school children working on computers, I wonder about their parents, many of whom cannot read the want ads in the newspaper and, if they could, would not have the minimum requirements for the jobs advertised.

Elderly Homelessness

There is also the tragedy of the elderly homeless. Some of the people have lost their own children, or never had any. As they age, they move out of jobs and try to subsist on social security which, especially for women, is often minimal. As Congress talks of cuts in Medicare, many elderly worry about how they will survive. The luckiest are those who own a home and no longer have mortgage payments. However, even these lucky ones still have to pay taxes. They also have to pay for heat, electricity, water, food, and medicines. The overwhelming and heart-breaking choices between heat and food, or food and medicine, can become a factor in the mental breakdown of these people. The frail elderly are a part of the homeless population which is as painful to see as the homeless children wandering in our city parks. Widows are especially at risk, since with the death of their spouses their own social security benefits frequently fall below what is needed to survive.

One of our elderly neighbors was clearly becoming less and less able to be on her own in her house. Good-hearted neighbors began talking to her about going into a retirement home. The parish social worker and visitor knew that the woman's income could not begin to pay for such a move. Eventually, some nieces and nephews came to her rescue, after having realized the situation which she, in her pride, had kept from them. Not every elderly person has caring relatives. Indeed, one of the saddest realities in many ordinary neighborhoods is the situation of elderly who have outlived most of their relatives and friends and who live in a state of constant fear.

Housing Deficits

A major cause of homelessness in America is the rapid decline of low-income, affordable housing. The reasons for this are multiple: the conversion of rental properties into condominiums requiring the buying of apartments that had been previously rented; the planned decay of many apartment buildings by owners who allow the properties to be condemned so they can then sell them to developers; and the failure of many of the high-rise federally funded housing "projects" which were neglected and degenerated into crime-ridden areas where tenants had little or no control.

The availability of low-cost housing for the lower middle class and poor has declined drastically over the past fifteen years. One of the major causes was the inflation of the 1980s during which the cost of all kinds of housing rose dramatically. The median price of a single-family dwelling in 1970, for example, was $23,000; in 1980 it was $62,200; in 1989 it was $92,900; and by 1993 it was $104,000. The cost of renting followed the same inflationary trend.

Abuse of Women and Children

A growing problem in the United States is that of violence: abuse of women and children and battering by husbands, boyfriends, and fathers. According to the FBI's *Uniform Crime Reports*, every fifteen seconds some woman in this country is beaten by her husband or boyfriend. In 1988, the U.S. Surgeon General reported domestic violence as the number-one health risk among women.

For many women and their children, the final solution to this situation is flight, initially to the battered women's shelter, followed by the long and patient journey of moving from dependence on the male batterer to independence. Some of the most successful programs involve transitional living facilities that help women to move not only out of a bad relationship, but also out of homelessness. Unfortunately, for too many women there is no battered women's shelter available, and the streets become their refuge.

Related Problems

While homelessness is a severe problem in itself, it brings with it an array of other problems which make the situation of the sufferers even worse. Being homeless makes job hunting extremely difficult. Those who have recently become homeless sometimes believe that as soon as they get a job things will improve. But things cannot improve if a potential employer cannot reach you, if you have no address or phone number to leave with your application, and if you do not even have appropriate clothes to wear when you apply for a job.

The same problems affect children going to school. Unless there is a friend or family member who can help out, it is very difficult for homeless children to go to school. If the children are with the mother alone, and if they are staying in overnight shelters, often the children cannot be sent to school because the mother can't tell them where they will be staying that night. Thus, in addition to suffering the dislocation of homelessness, children are cut off from another important institution that gives shape to their lives.

Homeless people have great difficulty accessing healthcare. In the most dire straits, they go to the nearest hospital emergency room, where there is no possibility for needed follow-up. If the children are in school and become ill, there is no way for the school to contact the parents. Even welfare benefits and AFDC payments become impossible when the family is homeless. There is no address to use on their application, no address to which the money can be sent. Many of the early shelters tried valiantly to provide an "address" for the people they served, with relatively little success. So a cycle develops in which people are caught, homeless because of no job, jobless because of no home. The cycle leads to growing despair, and sometimes to abandonment of the children in the hope that somehow they will be better off. This splitting of families was one of the major factors in the development of the transitional living facilities mentioned above.

The weather in much of the northern part of the country adds to the suffering of the homeless in winter. While children may laugh at the homeless man or woman wearing layers of clothing, several coats, etc., the cold winters can kill. I have seen homeless people sitting on vents in streets to warm themselves. At night homeless adults bundle into doorways with all of their belongings, trying to sleep in below-freezing weather. More than one city has resorted to arresting the homeless when the temperature goes below freezing, only to release them the next day. The headlines that scream about homeless people freezing to death on the streets of a city have not only moral, but also political, consequences that can bring about action.

Probably the worst problem for homeless people is that the routes out of homelessness are closed to them because they are homeless. Training programs and job counseling often require that applicants have an address. The very strategies that could help are not available to the most seriously deprived people. All of these problems, in addition to the reality of homelessness itself, have led to creative solutions which are dealt with later in this chapter.

STRATEGIES THAT DON'T WORK

Stop Gap Measures
As social situations reach crisis levels, societies usually respond with stop gap measures. These measures do not work in the long term. In the early years, as awareness of homelessness as a major problem grew, certain ameliorative measures were taken. They were often initiated by religious groups, churches, reli-

gious communities, and individuals who were touched by the plight of those suffering. Many parishes opened soup kitchens or food pantries, and sponsored clothing drives and programs of meals for poor elderly in the parish. While many of these were well intentioned, and helped in an immediate way, they were failed strategies in the sense that they touched only the results of homelessness, not the causes.

Criminalization

Too often the response of cities has been to treat homelessness as a crime. The homeless can be arrested for vagrancy, for panhandling, for loitering around certain areas, for using public facilities in railroad stations and libraries. In most cases, they are released from jail the next day, perhaps worse off for having spent the night locked in with actual criminals.

The Overnight Shelter

As the size of the problem became apparent, and the numbers of homeless grew, many cities set up large overnight shelters where the homeless could check in at the end of the afternoon, but had to check out the following morning. This same strategy was used during the Great Depression of the 1930s. In some cities, the homeless were arrested at night and released in the morning simply as a way of eliminating the sight of them sleeping in the streets. Sometimes it is hard to tell the difference between the overnight shelter and the city lock-up. There have been many books, articles, and even TV programs which recount some of the horrors experienced by women in large city-run shelters: battering, rape, theft, not just by other homeless but often by the guards who are supposed to be protecting them. At their best, what overnight shelters provide is supper, possibly a shower, a bed, and breakfast before turning people back out on the streets in the morning. There are many stories of women who, though sick, still were made to leave in the morning.

Soup Kitchens

Soup kitchens and the lines outside them were a regular sight in the 1930s. What is different now is that many of those who line up are women and children, sometimes whole families. Eating in a soup kitchen is a necessary measure to avoid starvation. However, often it adds to the sense of failure and hopelessness for many of the homeless.

Even when shelters and soup kitchens are run by religious groups with a great deal of compassion and care, they are still not a solution. Gradually, many shelters began experimenting with day programs so that the homeless could stay inside during cold weather. The frustration of those who were working with the homeless began to move them toward other actions, such as political protesting for more and better help from government at the local and federal level, and to new approaches that would provide not simply a place to stay at night, but also a way out of homelessness.

STRATEGIES THAT WORK

As is often the case, religious groups were among the first to begin to look for alternatives to the overnight shelters and the problems brought about by them. As parishioners and volunteers in shelters and soup kitchens saw the real situation and the system failures, they were deeply shocked. For some middle-class people, the shock was so great that they walked away and never looked back. Others determined to find workable alternatives. What follows are some of the alternatives, both those tried and proving successful, and others which are still to be tried.

Different Kinds of Shelters
Many Catholic sisters were in the vanguard of the movement to create a new kind of shelter. They started with small efforts. As their awareness of the size of the problem grew, more elaborate plans began to be made.

The first attempts by religious women included efforts to set up small shelters—similar to group homes—for women and children. They were actually ordinary houses with three to five bedrooms where women could come with their children and stay while they tried to get their lives back together. These simple shelters provided someplace to live, regular meals, clothing, and a safe space for the children while the mother looked for work or for longer-term assistance. The shelters were initially set up for battered women who had fled an abusive husband or boyfriend. Gradually, however, they were opened to any women and children needing assistance. These homes also put the women in touch with various other agencies, such as community mental health centers which could provide counseling or welfare offices where they could apply for AFDC and other benefits.

The Kitchen in Springfield, Missouri, which is supported by fifty area churches as well as a $1 million grant from HUD, provides short-term housing in a former hotel as well as longer-term transitional housing in furnished apartments for up to eighteen families. The program includes access to a medical and dental clinic, a pharmacy, and a day care center, as well as parenting classes, drug rehab counseling, and GED classes. This combination of short- and long-term assistance is found in many of the newer strategies.

Transitional Housing

Short-term shelters were often successful in helping people who were able to get on their feet in a relatively short time. For others—battered women, people with long-term deficits in education and training, welfare mothers trying to get out of the system—there was a need for a different approach, the transitional living approach. An increasing number of transitional living programs are being developed around the country.

Dreuding Center Project Rainbow, run by the Holy Redeemer Health System in Philadelphia, is a good example of collaboration between a religious congregation and a health system. The sisters wanted to do something which would have long-term effects for homeless women and children. The transitional housing project that they started provides much more than simply housing. The women have opportunities to complete their high school education and enroll in training programs for jobs. School-age children go to local schools and preschoolers take part in the center's own day care program. Part of the work of the women while they are there is to learn the necessary skills for making it on their own when they leave Project Rainbow. The health system, in addition to contributing major funding, also provides health assistance to the families.

The Transitional Living Center project was founded by Dominican Sisters in Spokane, Washington, and is now co-sponsored by four congregations in the area. Like others, they started with a house which they owned in the city and focused first on women and then on women and children. The drawbacks of a group living setting became obvious to them very quickly. While better than a shelter, a group home does not foster independence. The center is now housed in a building with sixteen complete one- to three-bedroom apartments where thirty-five to forty women and children can be accommodated. The program, which serves homeless single women with one to three children under ten years of age, offers counseling, on-site child care, basic life skills training, healthcare, transportation, education, and training in employment seeking skills and parenting skills. The center works in collaboration with existing social service agencies. At an assembly which the sisters held several years ago, some of the women asked if they could come and thank the sisters for their help. The stories they told were very frank and moving.

Project H.O.M.E. (Housing, Opportunities, Medical Care, Education) was begun by the same Sisters of Mercy in Philadelphia who had been arrested for taking coffee and sandwiches to the homeless in Philadelphia train stations. The mission statement of this project speaks to the heart of the matter: "We commit ourselves to forming a Community of Hope, drawing its members from all walks of life, to respond to the needs of chronically homeless men and women of Philadelphia." One of its first housing efforts was the conversion of a closed Catholic school into long-term housing for homeless mentally disabled women. The sisters now have an array of housing options for men, women, and children, including short-term and long-term apartment living. They have involved many other caring organizations and individuals in helping the people they serve prepare for re-entry into the mainstream. The emphasis is on enabling people to achieve the best that is possible in a humane and dignified way. Job counseling is a key element in all of the work of the H.O.M.E. group. Permanent specialized housing for the mentally disabled continues to be a key part of the program.

In addition, the sisters have started a number of auxiliary projects. One such is the Back H.O.M.E. Cafe, a restaurant that trains people in food service while providing a catering service to other organizations in the city. The Cornerstone Community Book & Art Center sells books focusing on ecumenical, spiritual, theological, social justice, and peace issues while providing employment for formerly homeless persons. Additional projects include: forty-eight units of permanent housing for men and women with special needs; Our Daily Threads Thrift Store, which supplies both employment and good clothes at low cost; and Seeds of Hope, an after-school program for children in the neighborhood.

H.O.M.E. has been an outstanding example of involving all segments of the community in dealing with a community situation. While begun by religious women, it soon involved many lay volunteers as well as other religious people. It also reached out to the city administration and to various state and federal agencies, calling attention to the rights of the homeless as citizens of the country. Foundations and corporations have been drawn in as well. The many successes of this particular effort demonstrate some of the best qualities of the strategies that work: a clear sense of mission, a focus on longer-term causes and, consequently, on longer-term responses, and a collaborative approach.

Affordable Housing Initiatives
Since one of the long-term causes of homelessness is the decline in affordable and low-income housing, it is obvious that one critical strategy is to provide such housing. Over the last few years there has been growing concern over the problems plaguing large high-rise "projects" built to provide low-income housing. Responses to this concern have included attempts at rehabilitating the decrepit buildings, initiating crime prevention measures within the projects, and empowering the residents themselves. The picture usually seen on television, however, is that of the implosive destruction of the buildings.

Some cities have focused on rehabilitation of the physical plants, combined with greater involvement of the residents in housing management. This has required some training. While this approach has produced significant successes, they have primarily been in smaller housing developments with relatively low population densities.

The strategies that are most productive are those which eventually make ownership of the property a possibility for those who live there. As long as people are in a dependent mode, the chances for long-term change are lessened. An exception would be in apartment living where the arrangements are similar to those in a co-op, so that people know they actually do have a say in how things function where they live.

A growing area of success is in combined efforts that bring together the private sector, the religious sector, and the government to actually build new housing that is focused on the low-income population and the elderly poor.

CommonBond Communities in Minneapolis is one of the successful strategies. This effort is the result of an affiliation between the Catholic archdiocese of St. Paul and Minneapolis. At present it is one of the largest private, non-profit community development corporations working in the area of housing. Its emphasis is on low-income and elderly access to housing. Since its founding in 1974, it has sponsored and now owns more than $70 million in housing, including more than 2,000 units in eighteen Minnesota communities.

In Denver, Colorado, Mercy Housing, Inc. (MHI) is another example of a successful housing initiative which goes to the core of the need for housing for low- and very-low-income people. It has developed and operates multi-family rental housing in ten western states. Sponsored by the Auburn, Burlingame, Cedar Rapids, and Omaha communities of the Sisters of Mercy and the Sisters of St. Joseph of Peace, it has created over twelve hundred units of affordable housing since 1987. MHI's Mercy Loan Fund has been capitalized with six million dollars of no- or low-interest rate investments from religious congregations, and is able to underwrite loans for affordable housing projects. It has made possible affordable housing for 8,000 people.

These two projects, and others like them around the country, show how collaborative efforts of non-profit groups can lead to positive results in creating and sustaining community-based housing. Backed by federal and local funding, non-profit organizations can become involved in the building or renovating of existing housing, renting out the units, and managing their development. Because there is no necessity to make a profit, rents can be set at considerably lower levels than in the private sector.

A federal housing initiative could also make significant sums of money available to non-profit organizations for the express purpose of providing low-income and affordable housing. Legislation for just such a comprehensive housing program has been drafted by Congressman Ron Dellums of California. The passage of this or similar legislation would be a sign of a genuine commitment by the government to meeting the housing needs of the people.

Urban Homesteading
During the time of the movement west, many people who left the crowded cities of the East and Midwest found a start toward owning homes and farms through a government program of "homesteading." People were given land and told that after they had worked it for a period of time it would become theirs. While the injustices done to Native Americans in this particular situation cannot be ignored, the strategy itself has some merit.

Whole neighborhoods in many of our large cities are suffering the blight of abandoned properties. Some of these are taken over by the city when the owners have clearly abandoned them and defaulted on taxes. In other cases, the properties are bought by the city and rehabilitated for housing. This housing is then sold to homeless people who have qualified as potential homeowners; they are a new generation of homesteaders. This approach helps not only the family, but also the neighborhood, which trades abandoned buildings for family owned homes, and the city, which sees a major improvement in the reduction of homelessness, the removal of blight housing, and the reclamation of devastated neighborhoods which can so often become the centers of crime. In some cities, "crack" houses are being taken over, renovated so that housing can be made available to people who need it.

The same type of thing has occasionally been done by developers, but this has led to "gentrification" of old parts of a city, providing housing for the upper middle class and more affluent people. Society Hill, an old and historical section of Philadelphia, underwent this kind of restoration movement thirty or more years ago. While this area is now a beautified addition to the city, it was redeveloped at a great cost: the loss of homes by many poorer people.

Rehabilitation of Housing

Rehabilitating older houses that are solidly built but have been neglected is another way of providing housing at much lower cost than erecting large housing projects in the style of the buildings now being torn down. Here too the collaboration of the private and religious sectors with city government can create long-term solutions to the problems of homelessness. Those who benefit from such initiatives are also, in a way, "homesteaders." Supported by other programs that help previously homeless people find work, they are given the opportunity to gradually buy the properties, build equity, and move firmly away from dependence on welfare.

H.O.M.E., mentioned above, has been involved in just such an effort in Philadelphia. Its housing programs, and others like it, refurbish abandoned houses or badly deteriorated properties to revitalize parts of the city as well as assist those who need homes. Habitat for Humanity has been demonstrating for years the workability of programs that involve the needy in rehabilitating what will eventually become their property.

A number of programs in colleges and churches provide for short-term involvement of young people in this work. The experience often has life-changing effects on the students who work on these projects. Christmas in April is co-sponsored by the Wharton School of Business and the Orleans Technical Institute in Philadelphia. Each year during spring break students have the opportunity to work in a housing rehabilitation project. As they meet and work with the people who will move into the houses they experience a type of community involvement that has more value than a "fling" in Florida.

House Sharing

There are a number of local programs that help the elderly to share housing. Often a single elderly person is living in a home bought years before, now too large for one person. The reluctance to sell and move is sometimes related to fear of losing contact with friends and neighbors. When people sell and move to apartments outside their original neighborhoods in the city, they often find that everything—shopping, church, banking—becomes more difficult because of the lack of transportation. While not a solution for everyone, the concept of sharing housing is growing in popularity and organizations like A.A.R.P. are providing innovative and useful models.

Home sharing could be at least an interim possibility for some homeless families if counseling is provided and individuals and families are well matched. A number of religious congregations began their work with the homeless by opening up some of their houses for such sharing. Just as some people have enriched their lives by being foster parents to children, others may find that becoming a foster family to others can also be an enriching experience.

Financial Approaches

In many cities, families find it hard to get low-interest mortgages. Although housing may be available, banks are reluctant to give mortgages because of the area in which the housing exists. This is where the banking world can learn from the experience of Mohammed Yunus and the Grameen Bank in Bangladesh.

The First Community Bank of Washington, D.C., mentioned earlier, is an example of a bank that has decided to serve low- and moderate-income neighborhoods in the District of Columbia. Its plans include loans for mortgages, as well as work with community organizations to facilitate the development of affordable housing. Georgetown University has invested in the bank, and other religious organizations looking for socially conscious banking organizations may begin to do likewise.

Another possible approach is to establish special publicly funded non-profit housing banks which would be able to provide construction or rehabilitation loans to non-profit organizations at very low rates of interest. This would help to reduce the costs of building and maintaining housing developments.

Such an approach to the housing crisis would also increase the supply of units and keep them permanently affordable and in the control of local communities.

A Political Strategy: Refocus on Cities

A growing concern among many people is the apparent trend in both federal and state governments toward an increased abandonment of the cities. The post-World War II building boom that focused on suburban developments led to a flight out of the cities by the middle class. Some people moved because they were attracted by less congested areas. In addition, the building of a national network of highways made living in the suburbs more possible for those who worked in the cities. Without doubt, some of the flight was racially motivated as well.

As people left for the suburbs, the inner cities and gradually even larger areas of the cities were left to the working class and the poorer people. The flight to the suburbs resulted in the loss of the tax base which had kept cities viable for generations. Neighborhoods began to decay. At the same time, both the federal and many state governments began to be dominated by the people who had left the cities and who demanded more services and amenities for the newly developing areas. Most suburbanites still wanted access to certain services and amenities that come with cities. The downtown areas of many cities are still central in terms of the availability of major stores, restaurants, museums, entertainment, and educational facilities. Nevertheless, over the last twenty years, the massive growth of large malls outside the cities has led to a decline of business in the cities and the blight of a number of center city areas. As the suburbs have spread farther away from the center, the demands of commuting have also put a heavier burden on the public transportation systems which now extend farther from many cities.

During the last ten to fifteen years there has been a return to some parts of the cities. The attraction of the arts, the theater, and in some cases a rich downtown life began to bring the "yuppies" back to the city. The children of the suburban flight rediscovered the advantages of city living. One of the attractions of city life in many places is the renewed desire for a sense of community. The closeness of a city neighborhood brings with it the possibility of friends and neighbors close by who share an interest in the area. A very positive element for many city neighborhoods has been the increase in neighborhood organizations, block committees, crime watches, and the return of the "block party" as a way to celebrate being neighbors. In an age when many people are seeking a renewed sense of community, city neighborhoods already have the basic ingredients.

Some city administrations are beginning to bring pressures on federal and state government to refocus their energies and monies on the rebirth of the urban world. One advocate's idea for renewing interest and concern in cities may seem utopian, but it has within it the seeds of a new vision. Doug Timmer advocates a policy of massive intervention by both regional and federal governments for rebuilding urban areas; he sees this policy as rivaling the Marshall Plan, which rebuilt Europe after World War II. It is a strategy that has worked in the past, and in some small ways is again working today as cities consciously reinvest in housing, roads, and economic renewal. The federal government's Empowerment Zones provide one example of how government can help in revitalizing city neighborhoods.

Another example, while smaller, points to the collaborative stance that is essential if the cities are to be reclaimed, if housing is to be provided so that large numbers of poor people and the elderly do not end up as street people. This is the story of two buildings on Manhattan's East 101st Street where Cecily Tyson grew up. The buildings were being allowed to decay and were on the verge of being torn down. Through the collaborative efforts of one man, the city of New York, and the SFDS Development Corporation (a coalition of three East Harlem churches), these buildings and two other abandoned tenements were rehabilitated into housing for fifty-eight low-income and homeless families.

The Sisters of Mercy have joined in another public/private drive initiated by the federal government to increase the rate of home ownership by women. Through their McAuley Institute, a national non-profit housing development association, the sisters are collaborating with groups that provide low-income housing. This particular effort is aimed at reducing discrimination against women as home owners by the lending market.

A Political Strategy: Regionalization

It is gradually becoming more apparent that the separation of cities and suburbs into two totally independent entities is a fiction. Cities, no matter how poor they are, provide certain services and amenities that are essential for suburban life. Many businesses and corporate headquarters are located within cities. Suburbanites, with relatively few exceptions, work in the cities, commuting to them daily via city roads or city transit systems.

In 1996 a major newspaper in Philadelphia did a massive study to look into potential benefits of greater regionalization. Philadelphia is a large city surrounded by extensive suburbs and many small towns. The study highlighted just how interconnected the whole region is. The interdependence is real, even if not always willingly recognized or honored. The study's final stage involved getting input from people throughout the region. As could be expected, many from the suburban areas were resistant to the idea that "their money" would be used to revitalize the city.

As long ago as 1984, Jane Jacobs wrote of the importance of thinking in terms of metropolitan bioregions, of metropolitan centers that are politically and economically integrated with the surrounding areas. This would help to foster healthy political and social involvement by everyone. It would provide the suburban middle class with a positive way to relate to the city rather than continuing to see themselves as in a fortress fighting off the infringements of the city. Regionalization is one way to improve the quality of life throughout the metropolitan area. Building on the basic interdependence that already exists, the economic system could be restructured to meet major social, financial, and human needs.

A Political Strategy: Tax Incentives

Governments at all levels can also be of help by providing tax incentives to those who contribute significantly to the availability of low-cost and affordable housing. Our present tax code often rewards property owners who allow their properties to deteriorate and eventually be written off. The property owners can then sell the properties for other purposes, and when the government lowers the capital gains tax, they are again rewarded for actions which have negatively impacted the whole community. Most tax reform advocates speak only of lowering taxes; they do not look at ways in which tax incentives could help ordinary people and the poor.

Special Services for the Homeless
In addition to the initiatives being taken to eliminate homelessness, many efforts are being made to alleviate the sufferings that accompany homelessness. A number of organizations have mounted campaigns to provide food, clothing, and healthcare to those who are still on the streets or who are making their way through the interim housing possibilities.

Heartside Clinic, a program of St. Mary's Health Services of Grand Rapids, Michigan, attempts to provide both primary and preventive healthcare for homeless people in the area. A storefront clinic, it offers free medical and nursing care, social services, health education, mental health services, and substance abuse counseling to the homeless. This is one of many health systems/church group collaborative projects to help the homeless.

Mercy Hospital, Springfield, Massachusetts, through Kidstart concentrates on the most vulnerable of the victims of homelessness, preschoolers. A case worker evaluates the children and links them with Head Start or other similar programs. Kidstart also deals with parental concerns. In its first year it served seventy homeless children.

Marseph, a program in Chicago, is co-sponsored by Marillac Social Center and Saint Joseph Health Center and Hospital. Both are sponsored by the Daughters of Charity. Recognizing that the major problem for homeless men is the difficulty of getting jobs, this program provides training in life and work skills to those men who visit a day shelter. Participants receive housing assistance, a uniform, transportation to the center, a meal pass for the hospital cafeteria, and counseling. The jobs they get are initially within the health system. During the six-

month program they receive additional training and at the end
of the six months they are assisted in finding regular employment. The program is linked to a number of corporations
which have hired the graduates of the program.

The St. Petersburg Free Clinic in Florida is a totally free
service to the poor, the elderly, children, and the homeless.
This program, which started out in a small house, has grown
into a major source of help for the most desperately poor people in the area. With a small paid staff and a large number of
volunteers, it provides healthcare for the most vulnerable of all
ages. Its services for the homeless include free medical care, a
clothing shop, and a food bank not only for individuals but
also for area facilities for the homeless. It has been actively involved in eliciting assistance from the whole community as well
as campaigning for changes in governmental policy at the local
and at the state level.

What is significant about all the strategies that work in
terms of homelessness is that no single approach alone is sufficient. The most successful approaches use a combination of
methods and rely on collaboration among various groups, government, churches, religious groups, corporations, non-profits,
foundations, and ordinary people of good will. While national
programs are helpful, homelessness exists locally and cannot
be fobbed off on distant federal systems. Homelessness, more
than any other problem, is based in the community and calls
for a community response. In our country, homelessness
should not exist. There are many reasons for it. The responses
and the solutions are also many, and there is a place for everyone of good will to be part of the solutions. The old proverb is
still true: "If you are not part of the solution, then you are part
of the problem."

CHAPTER 8

Mothers and Children at Risk: Violence

"Suffer the little children to come to me."
(Matthew 19:14)

What we see so often in our world today is not little children approaching a welcoming Lord, but the suffering of children on all sides. The horrendous pictures of children bruised and broken by war in Bosnia or Rwanda are paralleled in our country by those of abused and abandoned children, of young victims of drive-by shootings on our city streets, of angry teenagers violently striking out at others. Increasingly we see on our news broadcasts the unbelievable but true stories of teenagers deciding to kill themselves rather than continue to suffer. This last is perhaps the most dreadful of all: children on the threshold of life, children who should be dreaming of the future and of success, deciding instead to bring an end to life itself. Often these are the children of relatively affluent families.

Many adults find it difficult to understand and deal with the high level of anger found in so many children, especially in their teenage years. Youngsters who end up in juvenile detention centers and in the courts can often best be described as incredibly angry children. Their anger is often directed at people who do not see themselves as having done anything to deserve the anger. In many neighborhoods across America, the elderly become the targets of the anger. In some cases other family members bear the wounds of their children's anger. The high visibility cases are those in which children kill parents or parents kill or abuse their children.

We are a nation with many at-risk children. Where in the past parents had to worry about illnesses and accidents which could threaten a child's life, now they have to fear that their children may be the victims or perpetrators of crime, including murder, rape, and kidnapping. Several years ago, a young girl on her way home from a local high school was murdered by a boy almost the same age who wanted the gold chain she wore around her neck. It was a dual tragedy, involving two children and two devastated families. Children are killed for a pair of sneakers or a gold chain. They can be murdered simply because others consider themselves "dissed," shown a lack of respect.

Many of the homeless are children. In areas of poverty, those who suffer deprivation are children. Even in middle- and upper-class homes, the children of this generation seem to be more at risk than those of earlier periods. So many children do not have the support systems that buffered children in the past. The family has fallen on hard times. For many children, the extended family no longer exists, and even the institutions that in the past were on the side of children are now often their adversaries.

It is tempting to focus entirely on the children because they are so visible in their torment. What is hidden beneath any picture of a child is that of the mother. The people most at risk in our society, our world society, are women and children. We cannot place one against the other. They are bound together by blood and by the high risk of violence in their lives. In this chapter, I look not at women alone or at children alone, but at the two together. Throughout history, artists created many pictures of the mother and child. Our current world is producing more pictures of the suffering mother and child played out in a vast variety of scenarios.

The African proverb says: "It takes a village to raise a child." For so many of today's children the "village" now is the neighborhood, the city, the school or church, and too often the gang. In our modern world, all of us must create the village that we need, or we will not be able to raise our children.

HOW DID WE GET HERE?

Changes in the Family

During election years the politicians play upon the fears of crime, drug abuse, and the collapse of families. They talk in broad generalities of billions of dollars to fight crime, drug abuse, and family problems. They speak easily of the importance of family values and morality, sometimes with the implication that the problems have to do with failures on the part of families. The single parent, usually a mother, becomes the target of punishment rather than assistance. The two-job family is castigated for not putting children first. The idyllic picture of the 1950s TV sitcom family is invoked. No one seems to notice that these television families were white, suburban, middle-class families with two or three children, an extended family of uncles and aunts and grandparents, and a network of neighbors who knew one another. One might question whether this was a realistic portrayal of families in the 1950s. Without question, it is not a realistic portrayal of far too many families today.

Whether we like it or not, the extended family has been in decline for many years now in the Western world. Increasingly, the same pattern is found in areas of Africa and Asia. The close-knit family that featured parents with their children, surrounded and supported by relatives and friends, has been changing for decades. The disruptions of the Great Depression of the 1930s led to separations as families had to uproot themselves to go in search of work, often leaving the grandparents behind. Later the need to move the family because of work requirements added to the loss. More frequently today we find families leaving the "old neighborhood" for suburban life and older couples moving south for warm weather retirement. The time when several generations of a family were within easy walking distance of one another is long past. This is complicated further by the breakdown of families following on the large increase in the divorce rate, now believed to be 50 percent in the United States.

One form of the extended family that does continue is that of the teenage unmarried mother who stays with her family after the child has been born. Pressures from the government for such girls to stay with their parents in order to access financial aid are inadvertently creating a new form of extended family. But support—both psychological and financial—for the grandparents, who are often still raising their own children, is not there to make this new form more viable.

Another tragic example of the resurgence of the extended family is the grandparent(s) now raising the children of those who have died of AIDS. In a number of African countries, this is a new source of distress and poverty. I heard a young Ugandan woman tell of the deaths of several of her siblings. She spoke of how her parents, now at an age at which in their African culture they could expect to be cared for by their adult children, are instead trying to manage and provide for their surviving grandchildren.

The single-parent family is created by more than just teenage unmarried mothers. Divorce and death also create the same situation. In too many cases, especially among middle-class couples, divorce is followed by the disappearance of the husband/father. The loss of the father figure not only creates financial problems, but also gives rise to a sense of abandonment in the children and the anger that accompanies it. This can often lead to problems with school, loss of self-esteem, drug abuse, and sometimes even teen suicide. New government legislation aimed at pursuing the escaping father and ensuring payment of child support is only one part of the solution. The psychological sense of abandonment experienced by these children is not so easily repaired.

The two-parent family with both parents working is on the increase. Reasons for this are many and diverse. Financial need is the major one, since at certain economic levels it is not possible to support a family on one income, especially when it is minimum wage. The many women who have studied and worked prior to marriage and who desire, for a variety of reasons, to continue their double role of spouse/mother and working woman have both advocates and denigrators. Increasing numbers of children with two parents have limited access to both. The family structure with one parent home all day, caring for the children and the home, always available, is a rapidly disappearing entity.

Whether we see it as good or evil, it is a reality that affects families. We cannot legislate that reality out of existence.

The decline of the extended family has led not only to physical deprivations but also to the loss of support systems. The traditional role that grandparents have played in families is being lost. Even when grandparents could offer only limited financial assistance, they provided psychological and social support, especially to their children. Uncles and aunts, to a lesser extent, have provided the same kinds of support.

Over the last few years, the block party has had a resurgence in many neighborhoods. City permits allow the street to be closed off to car traffic, and people move outside for the day, cooking on front lawns or sidewalks, playing music, organizing games for the children. For one day, the block becomes an extended family, with neighbors as vicarious "relatives." This new form of extending the family, and of sharing the responsibility for children, needs to be encouraged and widened. Neighbors cannot be everything to a child which the parent should be, but concerned neighbors can give support and encouragement to children and to their often over-stretched parents. Elderly neighbors can become surrogate grandparents and wisdom figures on the block.

Violence

At the base of so much of the suffering of women and children is the pervasiveness of violence in world society. It might be useful to look at how we view violence. While the nightly news on TV mourns the victims of violence, and speaks out against the violence in our society, prime time TV, the movies, videos, and even video games in arcades glorify that same violence. The endless "studies" by the media moguls which claim no connection between violence on the big or small screen and violence on the streets simply are not believed by the ordinary people who live, work, and walk in those dangerous streets. The divide between fantasy and reality becomes narrower all the time.

One of the major areas of violence against women and children is that of spousal or parental abuse. While it has always been illegal, only very recently has any significant assistance been given to victims by the legal system or the police. In the case of spousal abuse, even some of the churches routinely blamed the woman, telling her that it was her duty to put up with it, or her fault that her husband beat her. Even today, the legal system becomes serious only after there has been major abuse, and too often after death has been the outcome. Systematic beating as well as psychological abuse is still a reality for too many women and children, and not only among the poor.

Children who witness or experience abuse are deeply affected and respond in a number of ways, from violence against the abuser to becoming abusers themselves. The son who sees his father beating up his mother may try to protect her, or he might learn that fists or bats are the appropriate way to control "your woman." The same lesson then is carried to the streets and the school yard where violence is the mode for dealing with anger, with fear, with "dissing." Children who have had long-term exposure to abuse of one parent by another or of themselves are at risk of eventually becoming abusers and thus moving the problem into another generation.

The very harsh reality today is that violence has become part of the fabric of our society. It is a systemic problem, but it is not being dealt with systemically. To see such a pervasive problem and to fail to approach it in a holistic way is to allow it to continue and to grow.

Poverty

The tragedy for women and children is that at a time when the extended family is disappearing, the assaults on them are on the increase. Poverty, violence, drug abuse, and the attendant health problems demand the attention of the often thinly stretched time and energy of the woman. The popular myth about women on welfare is that of the welfare queen in her Cadillac. The reality is that it takes incredible creativity to live and survive on the money from AFDC. In my neighborhood there are several supermarkets and a large discount food outlet. At the outlet prices are much lower, the items are not brand name, and they have to be tried to see if they are any good. I see many more food stamps being used at the outlet than at the regular supermarkets. Women exercise considerable ingenuity in shopping for food. However, many of these women live in neighborhoods where neither type of store is in walking distance. Without a car, they often have to depend on the small neighborhood store which charges more. Compounding the problems for poor women and children is the fact that major supermarket chains are increasingly abandoning poor neighborhoods.

In an interview, Marian Wright Edelman focused on the reality of the "child emergency" of children suffering the effects of poverty, violence, shattered families, poor nutrition, healthcare, and education. She has often claimed that as a nation we lose a child to abuse or neglect every seven hours and a child to guns every hour and a half. According to Edelman 2,800 children drop out of school every day. During the interview she discussed government plans to cut programs for children. The effort to cut taxes and balance the federal budget, she noted, was asking too high a price from the young rather than from the Pentagon, from corporate welfare recipients, or from the wealthy.

One great danger of the welfare bill transferring power to the states is that the women and children who have already suffered so much will be victims of variations among policies and practices established by different states.

Low Self-esteem

Women and children who live daily with the realities of poverty, crime, abuse, and constant disparagement by the press, TV, and politicians are not good candidates for a high level of self-esteem. Often adults are puzzled and intimidated by swaggering, threatening teenagers. Usually—but not exclusively—male, they strut around the neighborhood, menacing by their size, number, language, and even by their laughter. The impression they give is one of great self-assurance. The reality, psychologists have said for years, is that the exterior of the aggressive and overly confident person, whether child or adult, is a mask to cover deep levels of insecurity. The bully is often more afraid than the one being bullied, but the exterior behavior belies the reality.

When we get behind the false facade, what we find is a whole generation of young people who have grown up inse-

cure, frightened, and threatened. The flight into gangs is one
of the ways in which teenagers, especially males, find relief
from their fear, insecurity, and low self-esteem. Within most
male cultures, to admit to being frightened is not acceptable.
When one becomes part of a gang the sense of aloneness is re-
lieved, and the poor personal sense of self is replaced by a
strong sense of the power of the group. One of the significant
effects of a uniform is that it identifies someone with a group.
If the uniform is a prison uniform, it identifies in a way which
destroys personal value. If it is a police, military, school, or
gang uniform, the message is that the person is part of a larger,
more powerful, or safer group. Hitler understood the power of
identification with a strong group when he set up the Hitler
Youth groups. Studies conducted after World War II found that
many of the boys and men who were in the Hitler groups were
weak, fearful people who found strength in the group identity.

For too many young people, as well as many women in
poverty, the constant experience of failure results in a sense of
hopelessness, failure, and worthlessness. These feelings are un-
bearable for most people, and often lead to actions which convey the opposite impression. Children especially are drawn to
inappropriate and ineffective ways of dealing with anger, with
conflict, with the fear of failure, and with feelings of being
abandoned or looked down on. The killing by one child of another for a pair of sneakers, for a gold chain, or for a jacket is
less related to the desire for the material thing than it is to the
desire to let others know that the killer is powerful, is in control, can do what he or she wants. Rarely do children consider
potential outcomes, though for some even being arrested is a
way of feeling important.

Schools and At-risk Children

Compounding these problems with children is the suspicion or
even the sure knowledge that many of our public schools are
not equipped to deal with dysfunctional children and teenagers. The presence of metal detectors, drug-sniffing dogs,
locked doors, and security people on patrol in the corridors
are an indictment of a system which has lost the ability to help
damaged children. The level of truancy in many large city pub-

lic school systems has grown so high that there is little or no effort to stem it. When I was in high school, if I did not have a
specific class during a school period, I was assigned to study
hall and had to turn up there. Things are different now. As I go
past our local high school as early as nine o'clock in the morning, students are standing outside or setting off to wander
around the neighborhood. Some never go back into the
school, but hang out in stores or on steps.

These same children are often automatically passed on to
the next grade, and graduate as functional illiterates with no
preparation for the world of work. The years of schooling have
not helped them to cope with or learn how to live in our modern world. Children have become throwaways in too many of
our cities.

STRATEGIES THAT DON'T WORK

Prisons and Detention Centers
Many of our politicians run on platforms that offer to combat
crime—including the delinquency of children—by spending
increased millions on more prisons, more police on the streets,
and stiffer penalties including "three strikes and you're out"
sentencing. We already have more people in prison than any
other industrialized nation on earth. When we hear reports of
how much it costs to maintain one prisoner for one year, it is
hard not to think about the many other ways such large
amounts of money could be used to prevent crime. There will
always be crime, criminals, and prisons. However, there are
ways to prevent much crime, to reach out to children and
young people who are potential criminals and to help them become good citizens. While it is naive to think we will ever have
a crimeless world, it is more dangerously naive to think that a
major change in the crime figures will result from an expanded
punishment program.

Deborah Prothrow-Stith has written of the "deadly consequences" of violence among teenagers. She highlights terrible
crime statistics which show high levels of crime among poor
and minority young people and points out the failure of the

criminal justice system (strange name!) to make a significant impact. A doctor herself, she has determined that the model for a solution has more to do with a public health system than with a legal one. She is one of many people over the last ten or more years who have documented the failure of the prison/police approach to the problem of crime by children.

Prisons are often educational institutions for learning more about being successful in crime. Juvenile detention centers have become age-related prisons and fail in the same way as the general prison system does. Dealing with crime after the fact rather than looking at the causes and moving in a prevention mode is a road that leads to failure. The health profession has demonstrated for well over a hundred years that prevention is the best approach to disease. Diseases that were at one time major causes of death—malaria, small pox, diphtheria, polio—have been almost eradicated by the development of vaccine programs, swamp draining, and other methods of getting at the cause and either eliminating it or providing protection against it.

Violence is one of the highest causes of death in a number of populations. It is no surprise to learn that homicide is the leading cause of death of young black males and the second and third leading cause of death (depending on the year) of young white males. It is also a well-known statistic that half of all the victims of homicide are African-American, though they make up only 12 percent of the population. If the same figures were traced to malaria, to pneumonia, or even to AIDS, there would be massive pressure for research and for the development of a cure.

Casting Blame

Another prevalent failed strategy in terms of violence and crime is the simple blaming of the parents or of the children themselves. Just as parents were unable to protect their children from small pox until the cause was identified and the vaccine produced, so parents today cannot protect either themselves or their children without some help. While we look at children as perpetrators of crime, it is important to remember that they themselves are often the victims of crime. One of our politicians has suggested taking children away from parents and putting them in orphanages. This is the ultimate in parent bashing, substituting a rather benign prison for the more deadly jails. What this man forgets is that orphans are and were children without parents. The problem faced by children who perpetrate violence or crime is not that they don't have parents; it is a problem that goes much deeper.

STRATEGIES THAT WORK

When researching this area of concern, what struck me was that there are very few variations among the strategies that do not work. In spite of the fact that the criminalizing approach has been a failure for years, the variations on the strategy are few and mostly unimaginative. In contrast, the strategies that do work come in many and varied modalities, involving different people, groups, and programs. Not only do they work, but they cost much less than our large-scale policing and prison system. The strategies that work are preventive strategies.

Integrated Approaches

What is most significant about many of the successful strategies is that they tend to use integrated approaches. An integrated approach requires the involvement of all segments of the affected population, the ordinary people who are suffering as well as parents, educators, churches, businesses, government, and other social institutions. The collaboration needs to involve more than just the professionals. It needs to involve all layers of society, because all layers are affected and can effect change. Politicians, legal people, and health professionals can provide an overview and some knowledge, but it takes a wider forum *working together* to bring about change. Such collaboration needs to take place nationally, at state and local levels, and among all varied parts of the population. In the word of Marian Wright Edelman, it requires everyone "standing with and for women and children" to bring about the significant change that is needed.

A very interesting example of a comprehensive approach to violence that combines neighborhood action with the expertise of a health system is Youth Services/Family Focus Center of the St. Bernardine Medical Center of San Bernardino, California. This healthcare facility has moved beyond its medical services to reach out to the community by providing a network of community resources which address multiple needs in an integrated manner. Services include a parenting program, late night basketball leagues, job training, mentoring, a teen support group, an image/attitude program, counseling, and a resource/referral library. This healthcare unit is a true community resource. More examples of healthcare involvement follow later in this chapter.

Neighborhood Approaches: Community Involvement

People live in neighborhoods, side by side with others, and can choose to be involved with those others or to exist as if there is no one else around. I have lived in areas where the latter was the norm, and found it dehumanizing in the extreme. I grew up in a neighborhood where people were neighbors, for good and sometimes for ill, but *neighbors*. The approaches that have the greatest potential for success are those which take place in neighborhoods and which involve all the segments of the population.

The "village" that has to be involved in the raising of a child in our urban areas most often is the neighborhood. Where I presently live, a working-class area in a large city, neighborhood organizing has had a long and successful history. As neighbors we know that the way of life we want depends as much on us as on any of the institutions around us, whether schools, churches, or public service organizations.

Increasingly churches and church-run schools are providing for the after-school needs of their own children and others in the neighborhood. Many involve volunteers, teenagers, teachers, parents (usually mothers) who are available and can bring their preschoolers with them. This is a good way to utilize both school and church properties. A number of parishes have returned to the practice of making their spaces available for programs for teenagers. Public schools are a wonderful venue for such programs, though city budgets and the pressures of insurers sometimes block these programs. If some of these restrictions could be overcome, local public school buildings, which are among the most underutilized facilities in cities, could be used more by neighborhoods, their families, and their children.

In Philadelphia, St. Gabriel's Episcopal Church started an after-school program shortly after a new pastor, Rev. Mary Lainey, arrived several years ago. The program runs five days a week from after school until 6 p.m. The children receive assistance in doing their homework, and each day there is a special program in music, dance, art, or sports. The parents know the children are safe and benefiting far more from enrichment programs than from watching television or hanging out. Recently, the neighborhood paper *The Olney Times* featured a high school student who had attended for several years during grade school and was now spending several afternoons a week as a volunteer.

Sports as an Avenue

PAL, the Police Athletic League which for years has worked with children and teenagers through sports and sports teams, often uses space in church auditoriums or school gymnasiums of church-related schools. When a number of politicians mocked the idea of "midnight basketball" as a way of reaching teenagers and preventing crime, many of the ordinary people responded by saying they preferred to have the teenagers playing basketball under supervision than hanging out on street corners, easy targets for drug pushers.

In the late 1950s Incarnation Parish in Philadelphia built a gymnasium for its school. Today the gym is used every evening and throughout the weekend by a variety of groups who run sports programs for teenagers and young people. The ancient Greeks knew something about the development of the young through sports.

Many cities have a variety of sports teams which are organized within neighborhoods or slightly larger areas and play in local leagues. The sports activities themselves, the uniforms which give a sense of belonging, and the involvement of parents and other adults provide good recreation for youngsters while helping them build strong self-images based on the realization that people care. Local newspapers that print pictures of the young teams on the front page also communicate a message of support. Sports also help to develop a sense of teamwork, which is an important element in the process of growing up.

Recently, one of our neighbors asked a ten-year-old boy to go to the local store for her and gave him five dollars. When he did not return for a considerable time she was worried. Then the boy and his friend came back with the item and the change. Later she found out that the first boy had lost the five dollars on the way to the store and didn't want to tell her. Instead, he told his friend, who had some money and gave it to him. When she queried why another child would do such a thing, she was told they were both on the local drill team, and it had instilled in them a sense of taking care of one another. The happy ending to the story was that she walked with the first child over the route to the store and they found the original five dollars to repay the second boy.

Other Organizations within Neighborhoods

Many national organizations have concentrated on neighborhoods, recognizing the importance of reaching young people directly. One such organization, Boys and Girls Clubs of America, is an organization that has served inner city youth for many years. Its strategy has been to provide a safe, professionally staffed environment where youth are involved in programs that promote healthy self-esteem, positive intra-group behavior, and opportunities for problem solving. The neighborhood nature of the programs makes them ideal for children and teens today. Perhaps more than anything else it does, this group helps young people achieve a better and healthier sense of themselves.

Grandparent Programs: Many of the programs that are being developed in neighborhoods, sometimes through schools, universities, or churches, bring together two needy segments of the population. Seniors, especially those who live in the neighborhood, are invited and provided with materials to interact with children and teens in need. Some seniors participate in tutoring programs after school, concentrating on children who are having problems with their studies. It is an approach that helps to bridge the generational gap, and it helps both lonely seniors and needy young people.

Most of these programs show that, in addition to improving their school performance, young people grow in self-esteem as a result of interacting with seniors who convey their interest and willingness to help. In some programs, the elderly are also paid for their involvement. It may be only a small stipend and a lunch, but it is a help to those who are poor as they help others.

One such program is Senior Tutors for Youth from Oakland, California, which serves delinquent boys and adolescent boys and girls at a residential group center, and inner city children with below-normal basic skills. Utilizing elderly volunteers from a nearby retirement community, the program pairs young people with senior tutors one-on-one for periods of one to nine months. This leads to pairs bonding and discussion of academic, social, emotional, vocational, and personal problems. Both populations are enriched by the interaction.

Another program that is highly successful is Children of Mine in the Anacostia section of Washington, D.C., where one woman, Hannah Hawkins, has provided after-school support for children in a high crime and drug infested area. She provides homework assistance, a safe place to play, and supper five days a week. She runs the whole program on donations. What she instills in the children is a sense that they are loved, that they are important, and that they can become something. The loving discipline she maintains provides the only such experience that some of these young people experience.

Local Newspapers: In many cities there are, in addition to large newspapers, local or neighborhood newspapers. These concentrate on information about the neighborhood being served. The newspapers include information on events in the area, local problems and how the people are trying to solve them, and advertisements from local merchants, who often subsidize the paper through their ads. One such newspaper, *The Olney Times,* made a policy decision several years ago to include on the front page of the weekly paper pictures and stories about good things that were happening to and because of young people. Their coverage has included features on neighborhood sports teams, children winning prizes in contests, honor students in the local public and private schools, young people going to college or joining the military. The paper also covers the local public high school's annual "senior prom" at which the senior students, both girls and boys, take elders to a prom at the school.

In 1995, a large urban newspaper, *The Philadelphia Inquirer,* ran a series on violence for several weeks in its Sunday Op-Ed pages. The series included student essays about the upsurge of youth violence and letters from adults talking about the things that work in their own communities and neighborhoods. The emphasis was on encouraging people to become involved in neighborhoods and coalitions of neighborhoods, on helping parents, schools, volunteers of all kinds, but most especially on teaching the kids themselves how to deal more creatively with situations that can lead to violence.

Community policing is another attempt to bring together the law enforcement community and the community it is meant to serve. To be successful, this type of program requires the involvement of the local police precinct, the neighborhood organizations in the area, and most especially the people who live there. The community police officers receive special training in working with the people of the community. They *walk* their beats rather than riding around in cars, so they are visible to the people, and especially to the children and teens. Their role is to be a positive presence as helping and caring professionals. Usually they make special efforts to talk to the teenagers. If the officers do not receive special training and if the community and its leaders are not involved, it can be a massive failure. Through combined efforts, it can be very successful in reducing the crime and violence rate, and in giving young people a different view of the law. The officers attend neighborhood and block meetings, including block and town watch, and other neighborhood programs. They are doing more than providing crime prevention; they are also assisting in neighborhood development.

Conflict Management

Television shows, whether news or prime time programs, leave the overwhelming impression that the art of conflict management is being lost in our neighborhoods, our schools, our businesses, and especially among our young people. The young boy who shoots another because he has been "dissed" has learned only one way to deal with what he perceives as disrespect. Disagreements within a school that in the past were resolved with fists are now resolved with gunfire. The incredible proliferation of guns in the United States and the relative ease of obtaining them have made the need for teaching children and young people about conflict and appropriate ways of dealing with it much more vital than ever.

In the past what was not taught in the home about how to deal with and resolve conflict was often taught in the schools. Now, with so many schools, especially the public schools, looking more like fortresses, with guards and metal detectors, it is becoming more important than ever to teach the young how to deal creatively with conflict.

In many cases, what is at risk in conflict situations is one's self-perception, self-image, sense of security. Low self-esteem is increasingly being identified as the basis for much of the violence that is experienced by and among young people. The swaggering young male threatening others, the child with the gun, the gang members—all are living examples of the dangers of insecurity.

Some of the reasons for the insecurity of young African-American males have to do with poverty, non-marriage of parents, and family and neighborhood dysfunction. One program that attempts to nurture young black males is the Louis Armstrong Manhood Development Program in New Orleans. This program, using an Afrocentric approach, works with boys from age eight to seventeen to teach them what it means to grow into manhood. Traditional African male initiation rites are used. The creators of the program are convinced that it could also work with youngsters who are not African-Americans. It could be effective with whites and Hispanics, with middle class and poor, with delinquents and non-delinquents because it provides an extended family and community and provides positive role models.

While this particular program is designed for young blacks, the realities with which it deals are the same for many teenagers. The youngsters' lack of self-esteem is based on similar life experiences. It can be countered with a nurturing that aims to teach young people how to move from childhood through adolescence into maturity with an intact sense of self-value, one which is not founded on being a threat to others. Our society lacks rites of transition, especially for the transition from childhood into the adult world. The rituals of the past are either missing or no longer meaningful. Important research is being done to re-establish former successful rites of passage or to develop new ones which will help young people today. With the high drop-out rate in many school systems, even the graduation service no longer is part of enough young lives.

It is essential to involve young people themselves in reducing violence. Many successful local programs teach and work with young people in schools, churches, and clubs. A national approach is also worth considering. The Urban Youth Summit held in Washington, D.C., brought together forty high school students from inner city neighborhoods to generate new ways to respond to violence in their communities. They came from Philadelphia, Louisville, Milwaukee, Bridgeport, and Washington, D.C. The students worked on strategic plans for stopping violence in their cities. At the same time, they discussed the issues at the root of the crisis: poverty, teen pregnancy, drug and alcohol abuse. These young people returned home with a commitment not only to spread the message, but also to become part of the solution in their own cities.

A highly innovative program, Family Life Orientation Program, was started in Kasanga, Uganda, East Africa, by a parish in response to family problems related to battering and divorce. The program includes activities and classes on responsible parenting and child care. It also emphasizes increasing personal awareness, education for values, and leadership training. It now has twenty centers in ten villages and has expanded to include a health component with workshops on nutrition, hygiene, and disease prevention. This effort encourages people to work together to improve the life of the whole community by dealing creatively with their problems and with the conflicts which could destroy them. This Two-Thirds World community has much to teach our world.

Conflict management needs to be taught within our schools but often teachers do not have the special skills to do it. A number of unique programs have been developed for use within schools. One of these is the Community of Caring founded by Eunice Kennedy Shriver with funding from Joseph P. Kennedy Jr. Foundation. The program is used by 160 schools in twenty states and the District of Columbia. Begun as a program for pregnant teens, specifically to discourage repeat pregnancies, it focuses on teaching values and decision making to teenagers, using the concepts of caring and trusting, respecting others, and respecting oneself. Its aim is to create a community within the school, one that can help children to live and cooperate together. It involves personal discipline and a sense of belonging and of respect for others.

Another highly successful program is Educators for Social Responsibility Conflict Resolution Programs from Cambridge, Massachusetts, which concentrates on teachers, administrators, counselors, and parents, and offers programs, workshops, a curriculum, and resources. Both types of programs are needed, those specifically for the young and those for the many people who interact with and are responsible for them.

A local program which can be implemented in other schools is the Peacemakers Program of Conflict Resolution of Public School 321, an integrated school in the Park Slope section of Brooklyn, New York. Peacemakers starts with children as young as five and teaches them how to assert themselves and their rights without triggering aggressive responses. The children learn how to be assertive and civil at the same time, how to assert themselves without being either verbally or physically aggressive toward other children. As a result, the children are not only less likely to become bullies, they are also less likely to become the victims of bullies. A key element of the program is mediation by other children who are elected by their classmates and trained in the art of negotiating settlements.

A tragic area of conflict that has been growing for our people and our nation is the area of racial conflict. While adults often have subtle ways of acting in a racially intolerant manner, children and teens, who learn their attitudes from parents and other older people, have not learned to hide their attitudes. In multi-ethnic neighborhoods, conflicts often revolve around ethnic and racial differences: white-black, black-Asian, black-Hispanic, and other combinations. In some areas, where adults have made a conscious choice to live and interact positively, there has been much less racial conflict among the young. If it is present, we find that it has been learned in schools rather than at home or in the neighborhood.

A very powerful program to deal with this type of conflict is Teaching Tolerance from the Southern Poverty Law Center of Montgomery, Alabama. This program, which is aimed at curbing the rising tide of racial tension and violence, reaches over 55,000 schools and three million students. It won an Oscar for its documentary film. The award-winning video is sent free to schools which request it. The center also provides teaching kits for grades K thru 12, and a magazine, *Teaching Tolerance*, is sent free twice a year to 200,000 teachers.

What becomes increasingly evident as one considers the problem of violence is the necessity for greater community and parental involvement in neighborhood schools. It is parents who can call for specialized training for teachers who work with children in poverty and at risk of violence. Some of the programs cited above are easily available to schools, if the administrators and teachers want to use them instead of relying on police and guards. Successful programs clearly require the involvement of children themselves in understanding and working against violence, but they also require parents, teachers, and administrators who are committed.

Many private and parochial schools are trying to give more assistance to poor children in their neighborhoods, to those who are bright but financially disadvantaged or who lack the skills to deal with the violence that surrounds them. This is an area where assistance from foundations can make a significant difference. A number of years ago, the Connelly Foundation in Philadelphia made a decision to give funds to some of the parochial schools in poor and inner city neighborhoods in the city. The basis of the ongoing grants has been the demonstrated ability of the schools to do something good and creative for the children in these neighborhoods.

Corporate Involvement

Corporations exist in cities and towns. Even if they do not have a direct presence in poor neighborhoods, they indirectly benefit from the people who live in those neighborhoods and buy their products. On the whole, while corporate America has been slow to respond to its obligations, it is beginning to do so. There are a number of ways that a corporation can reach out to the children at risk.

Day Care: One very important and relatively simple approach is to provide day care centers at the workplace for employees' children—especially for the pre-schoolers, but also for after school care. Studies have shown consistently that when employees' children are in company day care productivity goes up, absenteeism goes down, and emergency departures during the work day are greatly reduced. Morale also rises considerably in companies that provide day care. Thus, a policy of social awareness and responsibility to the surrounding community and to one's own employees is also fiscally sound.

Adopting a School: Some corporations are demonstrating concern for the communities in which they exist by adopting one or several schools. There are many ways through which they can reach out to the children and teens who may someday become their entry-level employees. Corporations can help the schools acquire some of the materials that would make their educational programs more effective. For example, they can provide computers for classrooms in poorer schools. When companies upgrade their computer systems, they often find themselves with a lot of hardware they no longer need. Rather than burdening the trash collectors, they can donate these still usable computers to local schools. For high school students, companies can also provide part-time work experience that relates to school programs. These approaches help students to build an experience base and also to make career choices based on realistic knowledge.

Employees can be encouraged to provide community service through programs for area children such as tutoring, mentoring, or sports team coaching. Some of these services may be directly related to the kind of work the employee does in the corporation or to other interests which parallel the needs of children.

School Programs

School is a place where children should feel safe and supported. Unfortunately, for those children most at risk—the poor, minorities, new immigrants, and the socially disadvantaged—public schools often have little to offer. Teachers may lack the skills needed to deal with the special situations they now face. Yet, because these are neighborhood schools, they should be in the best position to help make a difference. Greater involvement of parents has always been one of the goals of most public school systems. Today, however, given situations of single parent homes, children with both parents working, or parents barely capable of coping with their own problems, the schools are frequently unable to count on the parents as they might have in the past.

For many at-risk children, the drop-out rate is also higher, so that they enter adulthood without the skills needed to make their way in the marketplace. Many neighborhood schools have reached out to other organizations and groups for assistance in their efforts to improve the life, the skills, and the futures of their students.

In the Philadelphia High School Academies a very successful partnership has been developed between the schools and businesses in the area. The program combines academic studies, occupational training in eleven career areas, and support from the business community in terms of financial assistance, managerial expertise, and employment opportunities for the students and graduates. The program has been effective in reducing the drop-out rate in the schools and increasing the post-school employment of young people. It also provides a supportive sub-system within the schools for those students who want to do well but can get lost in a large school where so many of the students are failing or preparing to drop out. Many of the programs used within schools to help students learn better ways of dealing with conflict help them deal also with other issues, such as pressures exerted on them by gangs, drug pushers, and their peers who have dropped out of school, as well as family problems and concerns.

Health System Involvement
It has already been noted that the reality of violence in our cities, especially among certain populations and in poverty areas, has led to questions relating to the public health dimension of this problem. As an expression of their commitment to healing, both public and private health systems have begun to address the situation by reaching out into the communities they are trying to serve. They have moved from simply dealing with the results of violence in emergency rooms and trauma centers to efforts to educate and to collaborate with groups working to reduce and end the violence.

The Peace Camp of St. Mary Hospital, Hoboken, New Jersey, part of the Franciscan Health System of New Jersey, is a week-long camp where children learn how to prevent violence. The program encourages children to find effective and peaceful solutions to problems. Recognizing the widespread nature of violence, the program aims to teach children alternative ways of dealing with anger and frustration. Methods include role playing, discussions, and skits that emphasize a positive approach.

Entirely too much of the violence that afflicts children is the result of abuse within the home, of spouses and of children. The Domestic Violence Task Force of Sacred Heart Medical Center, Spokane, Washington, educates hospital personnel to recognize signs of domestic violence. It also works with other organizations, such as police departments, schools, and HMOs, to identify and treat victims of domestic violence. Among the materials the group has developed is a brochure for battered women.

St. Louis University Hospital has started Hospital Response to Community Violence: HRCV. The hospital is a Level I trauma center, located in a poor downtown area. Its approach is two-pronged: first, it designs educational activities having to do with the message of non-violence for use with school children and populations at risk of becoming violent offenders; second, it provides holistic, ongoing support and education for hospitalized trauma victims. Other activities include educational workshops for parents, an annual Christmas party at local public schools to have children reflect on how they can contribute to peace in the world, and a toy gun buy-back program. Staff members work with patients who are victims of recurring violence. The program has also been successful in helping some teenagers move away from violence.

Providence Holy Cross Medical Center of Mission Hills, California, has set up a Violence Prevention Program that not only offers programs in the schools but has also been involved with the organization of a community coalition to collaborate on violence prevention. Community agencies, law enforcement groups, schools, youth groups, churches, and businesses regularly meet together. The program links up social workers with ex-gang members to offer alternatives to hospital patients who have been involved with gangs. This is another example of an institution working directly with the community it serves, and doing it in a preventive mode.

A well-organized program to help teens help one another is Teen Heartline for Help of St. Joseph Medical Center in Wichita, Kansas. Concerned about the increased danger to teens in their city, a group of people at this hospital organized a week of intensive training on how to help teens who were being affected by gangs, violence, suicide, and pregnancy. The group established a 24-hour hotline and advertised on billboards and the local MTV station. The hotline uses both volunteers and professional back-up support persons to talk to the teens and give them immediate counseling and information.

Violence, in the home or the school, on the streets or in the malls, is a plague which is destroying our young and corroding the very structures of our society. It is an American situation that we see daily, but it is also part of a larger reality which is world wide. Unfortunately, and too often, the response of leaders around the world is the imposition of even more violence—state-sanctioned violence. Whether it is death squads killing street children in Brazil, military troops putting down street riots, or police approaching fighting teenagers with guns drawn and ready, the message is clear. Our world is a violent one.

If our world is to become less violent it will be accomplished by many people of compassion, moved by a sense of justice, reaching out together to deal with the systemic disorders which are at the root of the violence. We don't need bigger prisons, longer jail terms, more police. We do need more people of every walk of life, in every neighborhood, banding together with caring professionals so that our homes, our streets, and our schools will again be safe and caring places. The effort will succeed only if there is a vast collaborative network of committed people.

Individual neighborhoods have taken their space back from drug pushers. Coalitions of neighborhoods can take back their city from drugs, violence, and crime and can recreate a space where all can live, work, and enjoy life together. The secret is in *conscious* collaboration, and the place for it to happen first is in the local community.

CHAPTER 9

Healthcare for All

"These twelve Jesus sent out with the following instructions:
cure the sick, raise the dead, cleanse the lepers, cast out demons."
(Matthew 10:5-8, NRSV)

We frequently hear of how, during his life, Jesus had compassion on the sick, lepers, the deaf, the possessed, a woman suffering years from a hemorrhage. He cured Peter's mother, the servant of the centurion, Jairus' daughter, the blind, the lame, Jews and Gentiles, men and women and children. Jesus' example has been at the base of Christian healthcare throughout the ages. Jesus responded to the needs of others whether they were rich or poor, slave or free, men or women.

Over the years, in different ways in various parts of the world, individuals of good will of all faiths or none have worked to improve the health of people and to create institutions and systems that can care for them. In many Two-Thirds World countries this meant shaping, almost from scratch, healthcare systems with a strong emphasis on preventive and primary healthcare. Many Western health professionals were very suspicious of China's "barefoot doctors," and of village health workers and traditional birth attendants in African countries. What was happening in Asia and Africa was planning for healthcare for the majority through simpler approaches and control of the expansion of hospitals and technologically sophisticated techniques and equipment.

In Western countries, government programs have gone from the minimal assistance of Medicare and Medicaid for the elderly and the poor in the United States to the comprehensive type of socialized medicine in many European countries and to the universal coverage of the Canadian system. The overall health of people in most parts of the world has improved greatly in recent years. Life expectancy has gone up in most countries and infant mortality has gone down. A number of diseases have been totally eradicated or greatly reduced. Although there was a time when there was great hope for the general health of the world, that hope has diminished. Healthcare is in trouble in many parts of the world due to some avoidable problems, such as poor planning, and a dangerous shift of emphasis from healthcare that is service-oriented to healthcare that is market centered.

In the United States we believe that we have the best healthcare delivery system in the world. We can point to major university research centers, organ transplant programs, and an ever increasing sophistication in our pharmaceuticals and technology. Yet when U.S. figures are actually compared with world figures, or even just with those of the major industrialized nations, the picture is not so good. We have an excellent system, with universal access, but *not* with universal ability to make *use* of that system, and it shows in our health statistics. Thus, American men are ranked fifteenth in the world in terms of life expectancy and American females are eighth. We are twentieth in infant mortality rates. Twelve nations have better cancer survival rates. In no major health statistic, except one, do Americans outrank people in Europe, England, Canada, or Japan. Because of Medicare, we do have the highest life expectancy after reaching age eighty. Some critics would say that we have the least comprehensive, most inefficient, and most highly technical health-care system in the world, a system which produces comparatively poor health outcomes for our population in general.

HOW DID WE GET HERE?

One of the key problems is that our access to healthcare in America is dependent on the ability to pay, usually through insurance, whether from government, employer, or personal plans. There are increasingly large numbers who cannot access adequate healthcare because they have no health insurance. In 1996, a number of estimates indicated that the uninsured or underinsured are in the area of 42 million people and that the number is growing. Those most at risk, poor women and children, lack sufficient coverage and what little they have through AFDC is in danger of being lost following the passage of welfare reform legislation and the failure of Congress to pass significant healthcare reform legislation.

We spend large amounts on healthcare, possibly more than any other society in the world. Although we have made significant advances, our healthcare is more *unequally distributed* than that in any other advanced industrial nation. The inequality of distribution is the central cause of the failure of the American healthcare system. Many of the countries of Europe are beginning to cut back on their socialized medicine programs. They can look forward to some of the same problems now being experienced in America and reflected in the statistics above.

While the major elements of the following analysis are based on healthcare in the United States, many of the same elements are creating problems in other parts of the world. Some of the problems are, however, very specific to the United States. It is clear to the majority of thinking people that there is a great need for healthcare reform in the United States. The continuing emphasis on the untouchability of the market, on the myths of self-reliance and the laziness of the poor, and a healthcare *industry* which is mainly unregulated except by insurance companies, all have blocked any true reform. The major effort made by the commission headed by Hillary Rodham Clinton never even received a significant hearing on Capitol Hill before it was dismissed. Yet many of those in the religious healthcare systems saw the work of the commission as very close to what is needed.

STRATEGIES THAT DON'T WORK

In a sense, the *whole healthcare system* in the United States simply does not work for too many of the people. Some parts of it work better than others, but even the religious health systems are falling prey to the same weaknesses and failures that plague the rest of the healthcare world. Public health systems are in even worse condition than those in the private sector. Over the last few decades many public hospitals have closed or have decayed to the point of being a mockery of true healthcare. The whole public system has been eroded by increased costs for equipment, medicines, and supplies, as well as by a constant cutting of subsidies from local, state, and federal government. Where it exists at all, the system upon which many poor people depended in the past is a ghost of itself. The other alternative for the poor in the past, the religious health system, is experiencing many of the problems of high costs, expensive equipment, and dependence on insurers, leaving it less able to care for the poor, which is, after all, at the heart of the mission.

What follows are some of the reasons why the *whole* strategy of healthcare in the United States doesn't work. We have major structural and systemic problems that undermine public and private strategies.

Unequal Access to Healthcare

No matter how equal we like to think we are, when we are sick we're not all equal. The sad reality is that access to top quality healthcare is limited to those who can afford it. When there was discussion of adopting a Canadian-like system of government coverage for all, people expressed fear of the dangers of *rationing* healthcare. In fact, the healthcare system in this country is the most rationed system possible: it is rationed by the ability to pay. We are touched when we watch the news and see wonderful examples of what our advanced healthcare system can do to help seriously injured or disabled children, sometimes brought from other countries by donor groups. At the same time, we have had epidemics of measles in our inner city neighborhoods because parents are unable to afford immunization shots for their children. We have seen great efforts to save the lives of conjoined twins, at incredible financial cost, while many other children come into the world damaged permanently because we will not spend the money to make antenatal care available to all women.

In the most humane of societies, healthcare is viewed as a right. The Judeo-Christian traditions that form the foundation for the American ethic would proclaim the *right* of all people to healthcare as basic. Now we see it becoming a *commodity* which we can have *if we can afford it.* No society can long endure that takes such a position. What is even more terrible in a country that prides itself on its compassion is that presently the largest healthcare gap is among poor and minority populations. This is quickly becoming the central healthcare challenge. Some of the disparity is related to racial prejudice and discrimination of various types. It is also connected to the marginalizing of the poor, a harsh placing of blame on the most vulnerable of our people.

The inadequacy of the present system is a consequence of its being based on a system of insurance that leaves out too many people. What we need is a comprehensive healthcare system that combines federal, state, local, and personal responsibility with cooperating community-based health delivery systems. Such an integrated system would be concerned with analyzing needs and distributing resources to meet those needs. It would recognize that, at present, people in rural areas and inner cities are among the most underserved populations.

While many women, children, and elderly in poverty are at risk—and will be so increasingly in the future as Medicare and Medicaid are cut or transferred to the states in the form of block grants—we also have elderly millionaires who can, and do, receive Medicare subsidies. The argument is that, because they paid in, they have a right to it. But this does not justify the transfer of needed funds to wealthy elderly who have other resources, while a few blocks away from them impoverished people are lacking the most basic help.

Lack of Integrated Planning
In the 1950s and 1960s as a number of former colonies in Africa and Asia achieved independence and statehood, they were faced with many needs. In the area of healthcare, many of these new nations had minimal resources, often only the thinly stretched health systems of missionary groups and the remnant of the colonial power's military health system. Ghana was such

a country when it achieved independence. It had at that time an internationally known expert in the Ministry of Health who recognized the problem and came up with a very advanced solution for the late 1950s. Knowing that the country could not go the way of the Western industrialized nations by taking the road of competition, he suggested a collaborative interaction between government and the existing, mainly religious, health systems.

The Ghanaian government committed itself to an integrated plan of primary, secondary, and tertiary facilities, with a role and some government funding for the private health systems. Rather than competing with the private hospitals, the government helped support them. The goal of the integrated system was to bring primary care to every town and village in the country, with secondary facilities (many of the missionaries' institutions) in larger areas, and with the more elaborate tertiary system spread strategically throughout the country. Although the success of the idea was often vitiated by other factors, including economic problems, the concept and its implementation showed a higher level of concern for all the people of Ghana than is demonstrated by many of the industrialized nations toward their own people.

The key to the Ghanaian plan was *integrated planning* for the whole country and all of its people. Such integrated planning has never been a reality in the United States. During the course of this nation's history, the healthcare delivery system has grown like Topsy, dependent on religious groups who built their own healthcare systems alongside of, and sometimes in competition with, public hospitals and a public health system viewed as primarily for the poor. In addition, as medical schools spread, university medical systems grew. The latest entry into the mix is the for-profit healthcare *industry*.

This lack of planning has led to duplication of facilities and services in large urban centers and to minimal coverage in many rural areas. Statistics differ, but most estimates indicate that as many as 50 percent of the beds in American hospitals are not needed. Unfortunately, the empty beds are clustered in cities, while in other areas there are not enough hospital beds. The unregulated and unplanned growth of the healthcare delivery system has left the country with too much in some areas and not enough in others. It has also led to a competitive mentality which has blocked the most sensible of collaborations. Even in the religious health systems, Catholic hospitals compete with one another for what is now referred to as *market share*, and other religious groups' hospitals do the same. The religious systems often compete, as well, with the university systems.

In addition to the absence of any national, state, regional, or even local planning, there has been an abysmal lack of setting of health priorities. With the advent of increasingly sophisticated technologies, this lack has had tragic consequences. We see complicated procedures to deal with rare and often terminal illnesses given priority over the much simpler preventive measures that have the ability to save large portions of the population. Organ transplants and other complex procedures are done to save underweight premature babies who might not have needed such procedures if their mothers had had antenatal care. At times there is the suspicion that new technology is being used simply to test it out, or to prove that it can be done. Science fiction occasionally shows societies in which the lack of planning over many generations leads to a situation where very harsh planning becomes necessary. In the fictional versions, it is invariably the elderly who are sacrificed. Tragically, in our own society—which is not science fiction—it is children and the poor who are sacrificed.

An area that is getting more attention, primarily because of the longer life expectancies, is the prolonging of life among the elderly and those with terminal conditions. Many people dread ending their days in a hospital, attached to machines, in pain and without the dignity of a family-centered death. The increasing use of durable power of attorney makes clear that this seemingly endless extension of life by means of artificial support systems is being challenged by the people themselves.

This is not to say that unusual illness should not be treated, or that organ transplants should be stopped. Rather, it is important for any nation to have clear priorities that cover all the people and all the needs in a way that is just and appropriate. We have too long ignored the plight of too many of the people.

The lack of broad-based planning and establishment of priorities has left us with areas of the country with too few facilities or with too many. As noted above, an estimated 50 percent of hospital beds are under-utilized because they are in overserved areas. Some have questioned the reasonableness of continuing the VA hospital system, one of the most underutilized, when veterans could be cared for in the existing empty hospital beds, and perhaps cared for better.

High Cost of Healthcare

The United States may have the most expensive healthcare system in the world. There are a number of reasons for this high cost. One is increasing reliance on ever more sophisticated technology, even though 90 percent of the illnesses that bring people to a doctor or a clinic do not even need the help of a doctor. In many cases, the village health workers in Africa who have had minimal training would be able to diagnose and prescribe for these patients. In this country we have placed high value on seeing a doctor, and on the use of very advanced machines and equipment. There are times when the doctor is essential, and when technology can help in the diagnosis. One of the disadvantages of the insurance system, and the tort system which allows for sometimes frivolous malpractice cases, is that doctors now feel it either essential or at least not hurtful to use a shotgun approach to testing for diagnosis. The art of diagnosis is being lost as doctors rely on a vast array of laboratory tests and machines. Some of the restrictions now being imposed by health maintenance organizations are related to what is perceived as unnecessary testing. Unfortunately, in the managed care environment, too often the doctor who has responsibility for the patient is out of the decision-making loop.

Since there is relatively little regional collaboration, every hospital ends up needing the same equipment and providing the same services as all the other hospitals in the area. For example, where I live there are three hospitals, each ten minutes by car from the others. Each has millions of dollars' worth of CAT scanners and MRI equipment. The possibility of collaborating or sharing is blocked by the market mentality and the competitive spirit.

Another problem is the under-utilization or total lack of use of some of the most cost effective measures, such as preventive healthcare, ante-natal care, immunization of children, nutritional programs, and basic disease control. While immunization is widely recognized as one of the most cost effective health interventions, poor children are often not immunized because of the cost of the vaccine. Poor parents frequently cannot afford the cost of the normal series of immunizations for their children. A national program to ensure the immunization of all children would result in a great saving in lives and provide a sensible way to reduce healthcare costs. Preventing a major illness costs much less than the treatment of it.

Approximately 25 percent of pregnant women in the U.S., most of them poor, lack ante-natal care. This can lead to premature and low birth weight babies as well as to medical complications for the mother. Some of the premature infants are born to teenagers or to other at-risk mothers, such as those with high blood pressure. The maternal mortality rate in central Harlem, in New York City, is 25/100,000 births, three times the national average. This figure has been traced to lack of access to ante-natal care and inadequate care at the time of delivery. Some of this is racially based; rates are higher among Hispanic and African-American women than among white women. The result is not only increased suffering, but also costly treatment for those babies who survive, and for the mothers facing complications of pregnancy that could have been averted through regular ante-natal visits. For the poor and those without insurance, there are few alternatives to the hospital emergency room. As a result, many women see a doctor for the first time when they are in labor and go to the emergency room.

Adding to these difficulties is the increased commercialization of healthcare as seen in the movement toward for-profit status of a number of systems. Shortly before his own death, Cardinal Joseph Bernardin reflected on the impact of this movement for the Catholic healthcare ministry:

> Our witness to hope is increasingly important in today's commercialized healthcare environment. There are strong economic pressures to pursue in-

come at the expense of the patient and, in fact, to reduce the patient to a commodity.... The moment we
shift our motive to one of profit, we will, in fact, undermine our primary mission. Few will find hope in God's
love for them if others make a profit from such care.

It has been demonstrated by numerous writers that the com-
mercialized medicine practiced in the United States is not only
far more expensive but also less efficient than that of those industrialized nations which provide care to all citizens. One esti-
mate is that 20 percent of health spending in America goes
into administrative overhead, some associated with the marketing of thousands of different types of insurance policies and
the processing of claims. High overhead is one of the reasons
for the infamous $5 aspirin on many a hospital bill.

While the for-profit health system is the most obvious example of the market mentality, the health insurance industry
has also put an increasing emphasis on profit. This is an industry that has too often tried to decrease costs by decreasing care.

While there are many great advantages to the managed
care revolution, especially in terms of its emphasis on preventive care, the danger is in putting profit first. A number of religious health systems have moved into managed care in order
to enhance their functioning while keeping their ministry primary. The risk of the market mentality in healthcare is in seeing it as a *commodity* which can be sold to those who can pay for
it directly or through insurance. However, healthcare is not like
a second car or a television set. It is essential to life and healthy
living and is therefore a basic human right.

Reform of the present system will require a moral revitalization which rediscovers health service as a ministry rather
than a business whose aim is to produce wealth for the owners
or shareholders.

Environmental Problems

The public health system was a pioneer in calling attention to
the conditions which create health problems or impede healthy
living. As that system has been reduced in size, we have seen an
increase in environmentally caused health risks. The emphasis

now is less on prevention and more on dealing with a problem only when it is well established in a community. Too often the problem is acted upon only after community advocates march on city hall, or the newspapers and television begin extensive coverage. This has been the case with some very serious conditions for children, such as lead poisoning due to the paints used in old houses and apartments. The damage to small children can be devastating, all for the lack of replacing some paint! Many toxic waste situations are remedied only after publicity and law suits, including denial both by companies and by government.

Crime and Drugs

A failure to deal with crime, drugs, and guns has led to a situation in which violence has become the major public health problem for teenagers in many parts of the country. Health professionals have started to recognize and call attention to the *health* dimension of violence. People in the area of healthcare need to explain ways in which they can intervene to reduce the number of victims of violence. An obvious avenue is that of public health, which historically has placed major emphasis on education and prevention. Twenty thousand homicides a year are clear proof that violence is truly a *public* health problem, and one which needs the attention of the health community.

Poor Nutrition

Poor food patterns are often found among the urban poor, especially the children. Sometimes this is due to ignorance on the part of parents, but it can also be related to insufficient income. The cheapest foods are not always the best for young children. The school lunch program and later the school breakfast program were an attempt to provide a basic level of good nutrition for all children. Cutbacks in these programs have had devastating effects. It has been documented that poor nutrition has much to do with attention deficits, poor learning ability, and even behavioral problems in young children. The food deficit problem is aggravated in many inner city areas by inadequate waste disposal. A number of cities have reduced their trash collection to once a week, and have eliminated separate garbage disposal, opening the door to many insect-borne diseases.

Lack of Early Intervention Programs

Three of the most serious problems that can occur in adolescence are: school-age childbearing, school dropout, and delinquency. All of these are conditions which can be prevented or greatly reduced by early intervention during elementary school through good health education, including sex and drug education. The number of school dropouts could be greatly reduced if there were more concentration on those physical and mental problems—such as dyslexia and low self-esteem—that lead to poor learning patterns. Few teachers are trained to recognize the early signs, even of something as simple as poor eyesight. School nurses are trained to watch for just such conditions. The child who is sleepy and lethargic at school may be lazy or may be undernourished. The child who has trouble following class work may be a slow learner or hearing impaired. If in the first years of school the child is labeled incorrectly, such a child is very likely to become first a truant, and eventually a dropout. However, many school districts and even whole cities have either eliminated or greatly curtailed the school nurse programs. The one attempting to diagnose can be the school secretary who has no health education background.

Teen pregnancy is a tragedy for the girl, for the infant, and for our society. Most sensible and sensitive sex education comes much too late for some of these youngsters. There has been some increase in good in-school education programs, but much more is needed. Drugs are available in many an elementary schoolyard. What is often lacking is very early education about the dangers of drugs. What is also lacking is training for those children who are targets of pushers, and who, for many reasons, are fearful of refusing. Often simply knowing how to say no, how to alert parents and teachers, and how to avoid the pusher is enough to keep children out of the drug cycle. Parents now teach pre-school children how to act if they are approached by unknown adults who are possible sex offenders or kidnappers. Very young children should also be taught about resisting the lure of drugs and the drug pushers.

Cultural, Language, Neighborhood Realities

Many healthcare failures stem from ignorance or underestimation of the impact of the culture, language, and ethnicity of a neighborhood on the life of the people. Given the long history of immigration in our country, this type of ignorance is surprising. Many of the newer immigrants are Asians, whose culture in terms of family and health is quite different from that of other groups. Language differences have been recognized for some time, and inner city hospitals often have multilingual staff.

Awareness by healthcare delivery systems of these elements in the populations they serve will contribute to the success of these systems. This awareness can be enhanced by regular and sensitive interaction between the people of the neighborhoods served and the institution doing the serving. As more health delivery systems begin to explore community outreach and walk-in clinics, it is essential that they meet with the various neighborhood organizations before finalizing their plans to assure the best possible interventions.

WHAT IS REALLY NEEDED

Primary Healthcare and Prevention

The single most effective way to increase the quality of people's lives and reduce both illness and the attendant costs is to make primary healthcare, or preventive healthcare, a *national priority*. In the 1970s North Carolina set such a priority, aiming to have a primary healthcare facility within easy distance of all of its people. At the same time, the Robert Wood Johnson Foundation made primary healthcare one of its major targets for support. Primary healthcare is one of the most cost efficient as well as the most health effective of approaches. Yet, it still takes a back seat to the hospital, the acute care facility. Too often the only primary healthcare available in an area is provided in hospital emergency rooms. Not only is this wasteful, since hospital emergency rooms have neither the time or the personnel to provide basic health education, but it also gets in the way of the true *emergency* services for which these places are intended.

An underutilized aspect of primary care is the use of other health practitioners in addition to doctors. Nurse practitioners, physician assistants, nurse-midwives, and lay midwives are able to do much of what is needed in 90 percent of the cases in which people seek medical care and in normal, uncomplicated pregnancies and deliveries. The training they receive prepares them to provide care and recognize those conditions which indeed require the services of a doctor. In many rural areas, the major primary healthcare work is actually being done by the nurse practitioner who is in phone contact as needed with a physician or a hospital.

Small town and rural clinics have been extremely successful during the past twenty-five years, but there are far too few of them in cities. Part of the problem has been resistance on the part of the medical establishment. As a result, people have not been educated and are unaware of what a nurse practitioner clinic can provide. In Greenevers, a small town in Georgia, it took a team of Medical Mission Sisters months to convince the people that they would get not just adequate but good care from a nurse practitioner. People had assumed that they were not getting a doctor because they were poor! They did not want second-class service. After a few months with a nurse practitioner and the occasional visit of a doctor, they began to prefer the nurse.

Need for True Healthcare Reform
What is most needed in the future is real reform of the healthcare system, nationally, regionally, and locally. Peter J. Murphy, addressing the Catholic healthcare community, identified four pressing areas of concern:

(1) creating a more rational delivery system in which the community's health needs are the driving force,
(2) building a solid bridge between physicians and the rest of the healthcare delivery system,
(3) ensuring that healthcare reform does not fizzle through our failure to provide universal coverage, and
(4) transforming Catholic healthcare from a ministry of religious institutes into a ministry of Christian communities.

STRATEGIES THAT WORK

General Programs

There are a number of very successful programs that deal with healthcare delivery across a wide spectrum. I have labeled these general because, in reaching out to communities and providing many services, they have a broad impact.

Inmed, of Sterling, Virginia, is a non-profit organization that works to enable disadvantaged people *worldwide* to improve the health of families and communities. Since 1986 it has established community-based programs in ninety-three countries. These programs work to achieve partnerships among public and private sector groups. Its decade-long Millennium conference series, begun in 1990, brings together experts from around the world along with community activists to look at what is being done in various parts of the world and what can be replicated elsewhere. The 1994 program focused on urban health challenges, and the 1995 program concentrated on children and youth.

Community Health Nurse Outreach Program in St. Louis, Missouri, a program of the Catholic Archdiocese, has placed nurses in five of the eight Catholic Community Service Centers. The nurses do assessments, health education, and health screening. They facilitate access to health services and participate in case management teams. Another effort on the part of the Archbishop's Commission on Community Health in St. Louis is the Parish Health Ministry Nurse Program which works specifically within parishes doing initial health assessments, screenings, and education. The aim is to help each parish fit its programs to its own needs. The program has produced a how-to manual for starting a parish health ministry, provides mentors, and links hospitals with parishes for better integrated care. Its strength lies in the community base and the linkage to hospitals.

Women and Children

In terms of healthcare, women and children are the most at-risk populations. The future depends on providing them with good healthcare. There are successful programs which recognize both the high risk nature of the population and the importance of making changes now. One of these, the Foundation for Higher Education, has been developed in Colombia, a Latin American country which we most frequently associate with drug lords. This program, which originated in a Two-Thirds World country, could serve as a model for many countries in the First World. Voluntary health workers from the community have been trained to identify and treat common maternal and child health problems. Workers are assigned to fifty or sixty families *in their own communities*. The workers are primarily mothers and grandmothers. They visit each family twice a month to provide health education and update records.

In Philadelphia, the Franciscan AIDS/Drug Baby Home is reaching out to one of the most fragile groups of all. Three Franciscan sisters act as legal foster parents to infants born to parents with AIDS or drug addictions. The "Sr. Moms" care for these children full time in a home setting. Opened in 1990, the house cared for twenty-three children during the first five years of the program. When, at around the age of two, the children who test negative for HIV are medically stable, they are placed in pre-adoptive homes. The sisters remain in contact with the children during the period of transition to the new home.

Head Start Program of Washington Heights serves a section of New York that has a largely immigrant population. The aim of the program is to provide education, health, and social services through parental involvement. High-risk families are taught how to function as a unit. The prevention and intervention models use lay involvement and community partnerships.

In the Watts area of Los Angeles, the Department of Pediatrics of King-Drew Medical Center is able to reach beyond its walls by training personnel for ninety day care centers in the area. The department collaborates with a magnet high school in health sciences which is on the grounds of the hospital. This provides an opportunity to interest teenagers in health science careers.

Another approach is the St. Joseph's Mercy Care Mercy Mobile Health Care of Atlanta, Georgia. Established in 1994, the program uses five vans and two medical units to deliver primary healthcare, social services, and education to 17,000 people. It services twenty-nine shelters, clinics, and housing communities and has a forty-six-unit residence for low-income individuals with HIV/AIDS. Key to its success is the collaboration of the hospital with other community groups in focusing on the special needs of women and children in the city.

In the Dorchester section of Boston, St. Mary's Women and Infants Center, part of the Caritas Christi Health System, is a diocesan-sponsored program to assist the neighborhood. The population is 49 percent African-American, 32 percent white, 15 percent Hispanic, and 4 percent Asian. The area has the highest infant mortality rate in the Boston area. Twenty-five percent of the population is below the poverty line; the median income is 35.5 percent below that of households nationwide. The center provides a number of interdependent services, some funded by the health system and some by government or other sources. It has been developed as a *community* program involving neighborhood residents, city and church leaders, public and private health and social agencies providing residential and healthcare services for women and children. The program offers education on parenting, health, and safety. It collaborates with the city in a short-term residence service for children in custody of the Department of Social Services. The program also offers comprehensive out-patient services in a neighborhood clinic, and provides counseling and help for victims of domestic violence. The integrated nature of this effort contributes greatly to its success.

A different approach is taken by School Health Partnership, an effort of the St. Joseph's Care Group of South Bend, Indiana. Two hospitals, St. Joseph's Medical Center of South Bend and St. Joseph Community Hospital of Mishawaka, collaborate with the Catholic school system to provide a school nurse presence. The hospitals train volunteer nurses to provide services to the six thousand students in twenty-one Catholic schools in the area. The schools recruit parents who are nurses and the hospital coordinators train the volunteers in conducting vision, hearing, and scoliosis screening, reporting communicable diseases, documenting TB testing, and providing flu and hepatitis vaccinations. Very important to the program is the emphasis on preventive health. It is a good example of collaboration between health systems, schools, and professionals.

Columbia University and Save the Children are collaborating in a program called Strong Beginnings, which serves children from birth through the age of three. The emphasis is on parent-child interactive learning, with special attention given to health, nutrition, family literacy, and family day care.

Pregnant Women and Teenage Pregnancy

One of the most distressing statistics is the high infant mortality and maternal morbidity rates in this country. The single most significant cause is also the one that can most easily be changed. Too many women, and especially teenagers, do not receive the necessary ante-natal care. Some of the following programs have significantly improved the statistics.

In the Granite School District of Salt Lake City, Utah, Community of Caring, using the approach initiated by Eunice Kennedy Shriver, provides a prevention-centered education program for parents and teens. Based on a values program, it provides for interaction with teens who have been pregnant and had babies; the emphasis is on the reality of having a baby, as opposed to the fantasies indulged in by many teenagers. The fact that parents are included in the program adds to its effectiveness.

A strongly community-oriented program is Friends of Moms of the Archbishop's Commission on Community Health of St. Louis, Missouri. This program trains local women to identify unserved pregnant women in their neighborhoods and to get these women early, continuous, and holistic ante-natal care. Of the sixty babies born during the program's first year, none died and none had low birth weight. This program demonstrates the incredible value of ante-natal care and the importance of neighborhood involvement.

A state-funded program of comprehensive care for those on Medicaid is Health Beginnings Plus of Frankford Hospital in Philadelphia. The purpose of the program is to reduce infant mortality by providing one-on-one support throughout the pregnancy of teenagers, a high-risk group. It also provides education in parenting.

In Rochester, New York, Healthy Moms at St. Mary's Hospital is a hospital based program emphasizing preventive care and early intervention for at-risk urban women. It also includes free child care, hot lunches, transportation, and help in preparing for employment. This program shows how a hospital can reach beyond itself rather than simply waiting for the pregnant woman to come into the emergency room in labor.

The Maternal Assistance Program (MAP) of Holy Spirit Hospital of Camp Hill, Pennsylvania, was established to reduce the incidence of substance abuse in pregnant women and new mothers by creating a bridge between perinatal and substance abuse services in the community. The focus is on case management, facilitating access to available community resources. Referrals come from various healthcare providers, as well as from county courts, probation, parole offices, and children and youth services. Clients are visited weekly in their homes and helped to set goals and become self-reliant. MAP also addresses problems with transportation and babysitting. It has had notable successes. In its second year (1994–95) it worked with 91 clients and in 1995–96 served 102 women. The strength here is the integration of the various organizations and services with a healthcare outreach.

Inmed supports a network of lay home visiting programs designed to reduce infant mortality and other risks facing pregnant women and families with young children. The network connects with clinics, churches, and schools and offers training for new mothers, which is especially important given the reduction by insurers of time spent in the hospital after delivery. MotherNet America is one of these programs.

Project MotherCare of the Hospital of St. Raphael in New Haven, Connecticut, is an attempt to deal with the seventh poorest city of its size in the United States. In 1989 New Haven had an infant mortality rate of 18.5 deaths/1000 births. The hospital turned a 58-foot tractor trailer into a clinic on wheels to bring ante-natal care to underserved neighborhoods. It also reached out to substance-abusing pregnant women, providing counseling, social services, and ear acupuncture as supportive therapy for drug abusers. Infant mortality at the hospital has dropped from 17.1/1000 births in 1990 to 6.25/1000 in 1993.

This is another example of an institution reaching beyond its walls to answer needs and simultaneously improving its own in-hospital statistics.

Health Services for Elderly Poor

The elderly poor are often forgotten in the area of healthcare. The widespread assumption is that, in terms of healthcare, Social Security and Medicare have removed the elderly from the ranks of the needy. Yet many of them receive minimal Social Security benefits, and cutbacks in Medicare have added to their problems. A major health-related problem for many elderly is poor and insufficient nutrition. Some senior citizens centers provide hot lunches for a small charge, but these programs do not assist the people who cannot get out to the centers. Several initiatives have been taken to help them.

In Philadelphia, Food for Friends is a city-wide program of meals for shut-in and homebound poor elderly. Volunteers prepare meals, or cook extra servings when cooking for families. The program provides aluminum serving dishes so that volunteers can freeze the meals. Volunteer drivers take the meals to the shut-ins. The major connection is often through parish churches whose social service staff usually know the needy in the neighborhood. Volunteers also visit with the elderly, which gives them an opportunity to check for other possible needs.

In Cape May County, New Jersey, Holy Redeemer Visiting Nurse Agency Food Bank is a full-service food bank which distributes food to poor and fixed-income elderly. It is supported by donations from local business and community members. While the primary clients are elderly, the program also serves single mothers with children living in poverty and families affected by job loss or illness. In addition, the agency runs a thrift shop that sells clothes and furniture at minimal prices, or donates these items to the very needy. There is considerable community involvement, since the food bank depends on the local community for most of the work of collecting and distributing.

Mercy Retirement and Care Center of Oakland, California, through Mercy Brown Bag Program collects and distributes donated and purchased food to 540 low-income elderly in Alameda County. It encourages seniors to help one another and provides nutritional and consumer information, referrals, and personal enrichment education. It collects about 750,000 pounds of donated food per year.

Project ElderCare of the Hospital of St. Raphael in New Haven, Connecticut, provides convenient access to medical care for underserved, inner-city elderly in New Haven by operating three clinics in local low-income public housing projects for seniors.

City Collaborations

A number of city governments have begun to collaborate with other facilities to improve healthcare for citizens. The Millennium conference of 1995 highlighted several.

In Washington, D.C., whose infant mortality rate of 21.9/1000 births was the worst in the nation, Mohammed Akhter, the Commissioner of Public Health, hired twenty-five illiterate grandmothers who lived in poverty communities. He sent them to talk to all the young girls in their neighborhoods, giving them reasons why they should not get pregnant, but also informing them that if they should get pregnant they were to let the grandmothers know. The city then sent a maternity care van out to provide free ante-natal care to pregnant women and teens. In one year the infant mortality rate dropped to 16.4/1000. This was a city-neighborhood collaboration, using the people of the area.

Another approach is that of Clinica Guadalupana of Horizon City, Texas, where the clinic is run by the Sisters of Charity of Cincinnati with donations of money and services. It is an example of public-private collaboration between the clinic, the public health department of the city, and the Sisters of Charity. It provides primary and preventive healthcare. In addition, it runs program TEAM (Together Everyone Achieves Miracles) working to build self-esteem among teenage girls, an important element in the prevention of teen out-of-wedlock pregnancies.

Another example of a program in a very poor Two-Thirds World country is the Community Mobilization for Health in Dhaka, Bangladesh, which aims to reduce mortality and morbidity rates among children under age six and women ages fifteen to forty-five. Its approach emphasizes prevention and includes immunizations, maternal care, nutrition education, and oral rehydration of infants. It uses networking among public and private sectors. A major focus is on education of local leaders in managerial, technical, and fundraising skills as well as in community surveillance of preventable diseases and pneumonia. The results are impressive: in the first year, 92.5 percent of the children were immunized and 82 percent of the mothers learned correct infant feeding practices. This is a bottom-up community-based program that mobilizes all socio-economic classes and develops neighborhood health committees.

One reality long recognized by healthcare professionals is that many of the most successful interventions result from institutions going out to the community. In many countries in the Two-Thirds World the idea of the doctor and nurse going "on trek" has had a long and successful history. Mobile Health of the Radnor, Pennsylvania, Mercy Health System began just such a move in 1996. This is a collaborative program involving Mercy Health System, the City of Philadelphia's Partners for Progress, and a major pharmaceutical company, SmithKline Beecham. The three-way initiative serves as a model for public, private, and corporate interaction to improve healthcare. The program began with one mobile van that went through poverty areas and neighborhoods to deliver healthcare to those with no insurance. The director of the program, Gloria J. McNeil, now manages a $1 million grant whose goal is to bring high-tech healthcare to underserved populations using a fleet of such vans. The mobile units provide a comprehensive set of primary care services including mammograms, immunizations, electrocardiography, screening, physical assessments, and counseling.

Healthcare professionals, aided by a host of volunteers, are reaching out to the underserved and neglected, using all the creativity, passion, and determination which has for generations marked the best people and institutions. The importance of the various religious groups and systems is paramount. Not only have they had a long history of caring for those left out and neglected, but they are a voice of challenge to the worst practices of the for-profit health systems and the increasing negligence of the government.

PART III

WHITHER NEXT?

CHAPTER 10

Why the Strategies Work

"The company of believers were of one heart and one mind...
there was not a needy person among them...
distribution was made to each as any had any need."
(Acts 4:32-35)

Much of this book has focused on the strategies that do not work and why they are failures. It is important, as well, to highlight why other strategies do work. It is only by studying the factors that separate the two that we can plan effectively for the future.

COMMUNITY BASED

Most essential to the successful strategies described earlier in this book is the fact that the efforts have involved the community itself, the people who are at risk and being helped. At its best level, this involvement includes the community in the analysis of needs, in decisions about strategies, and in the actual work. The time of doing things for and to people is past. What is needed for today and for the coming century is an emphasis on *empowerment of people*, which involves people in planning for and working toward their own destiny. Many programs fail because the experts, the professionals, do all the planning and the people are not involved except as recipients.

A good example in which I was directly involved was a primary healthcare project in Canada developed by Medical Mission Sisters with some funding from the Robert Wood Johnson Foundation in the mid 1970s. During a visit to the project team, I met with the provincial health director. As we talked about the project, he was enthusiastic until we explained that the board would be comprised of the residents of the neighborhoods in the inner city that the proposed clinic would serve. His suggestion was that the people could be advisors, but that health professionals should make up the board. We insisted on the point that the people served should be the board, because they would know what they needed. The professionals would be of greater help as an advisory board, since they had the knowledge to suggest various alternatives. The provincial health director finally agreed. That project is still going on very successfully, though the sisters are long gone to other areas.

The involvement of the community has to be real. It has to use all possible roads to community participation, from investigating the needs and desires of the people, through choosing among the various possible strategies. The people must be committed to the actions to be taken, and this commitment is possible only if their opinions are heard and honored.

A group of public health nurses studying in a master's program at the University of Houston had done a very good analysis, with the people, of the needs of a particular poor neighborhood. The two strongest needs that kept recurring were street lights and safe water. Naturally, the nurses wanted to start with water, since this was a major health factor. The people wanted lights first. The students' supervisor was able to help them see why lights were so important for the community: they would make the streets safer, and they would also demonstrate to other neighborhoods that *this* neighborhood was just as important as richer ones. Once the students helped the community through the process of getting street lights from the city, then the people were ready to make the major effort required to improve the water safety in the area.

In both the Canadian and the Texan efforts, the community was involved in the actions to be taken. If a study is done with a community, and then the solutions are determined by non-community experts only, the commitment will soon fade. Being involved in the solution as well as in the discovery of the need gives people a sense of their own ability and calls forth personal and group responsibility. It matters very little where an effort starts, as long as the community has a significant role. Neighborhood organizations can play a key role. When these organizations arise, they do so because of a real need. That need can be as simple as street lights, clean streets, or as complex as taking back a neighborhood from drug pushers. When only the experts are involved, success is at risk.

The police have seen the value of community involvement in their efforts to reduce crime in neighborhoods. As long as the police are viewed as outsiders, enforcers, the enemy, even the good people will be uncooperative. The community police model is one way of involving neighbors in increasing safety and reducing crime through town/block watches and community advisory boards at local precincts. The key is community involvement.

When a community is involved, solutions will include consideration of the ethnic, racial, religious, and cultural aspects of that community. These elements vary from one community or one neighborhood to another. The expert approach, whether it is a welfare department plan or a university project, may focus on the need, assuming that the need will be seen the same way by all people and groups. But this is unrealistic. What will work with one type of community may fail miserably in a different one. Without getting caught in stereotypes, it is true that Hispanics, and African Americans, and Asian Americans, and Irish Americans all come out of different cultural bases and act out of their own base. If the community being served is multicultural, then the approach has to respect that reality and those different people.

Essential to successful programs is people's awareness that they have power, that they can make a difference in their lives and those of their children. This is true especially in the case of those groups which have experienced powerlessness in the past, or who have believed that nothing would ever work. This is why it is important that the involvement of the community be real, not simply a facade. If it is not real, the program will quickly die. One of the most satisfying experiences for the expert or the agency working with communities is to see the enthusiasm that develops as people see that their efforts are bringing about change and that they themselves are part of that change.

VALUE CENTERED

There must be a sense that people want to make a better life for themselves and their children and that, given some encouragement, they can make things better. This is the opposite of the belief that says the poor are shiftless, lazy, and cheats. No program will be successful if it is based on a lack of respect for the people who are being helped. Often, though not always, professionals come out of a middle-class background and have a university or professional school education. While they have the professional tools and skills, it is important that they also have a belief in people and in their inherent value. Tragically, what often happens is that the young who come to help lose that belief if the system in which they are working is organized in a way that devalues people.

I remember sitting in a welfare office waiting room as a graduate student, watching how people were being treated and how they responded to the treatment. Each person had to go through several clerical-level staff, which involved moving from one line to another. The neighborhood where the office was located was a mix of white, African-American, and Hispanic people. Some had a problem with English and, as I gradually realized, some did not know how to read. As people ended up in wrong lines, or waited for long periods of time, you could see the hope fading, especially as they experienced the annoyance of the staff. Eventually I met with a social worker, who was very good and very concerned. However, as I left, I wondered to what extent the fact that I was a well-educated person, a self-assured graduate student, affected the way I was treated.

If any approach is to be successful, it will have to be based on certain values that are both held and expressed. Clearly, the central value is one of respect for people and their worth, regardless of their situation, problems, or neediness. Our welfare system in this country is a mixed bag on this issue. Sometimes when people are very poor and show it in the way they dress, their levels of cleanliness, and their language skills, they can meet with anything from disrespect to anger from those who are being paid to be helpful. Just watching the homeless on the streets or in bus stations provides a sad statement on how people are valued by the staff of the station, the cleaners, the police who come through, and by the passengers waiting in line for tickets or buses.

The virtue of compassion is essential in working with those who need help for any reason. This compassion is simply a recognition of suffering; it has nothing to do with any kind of evaluation of the degree to which the person is culpable. One can be compassionate without necessarily approving of behaviors that are dysfunctional. In many of the programs described earlier, what is most clearly apparent is the degree of compassion which was at the base of their beginnings and is at the core of their success.

Finally, a deep belief in justice is at the heart of successful programs. Those who run them must be convinced of people's right to live a humane and hopeful life, regardless of the experiences which have brought them to their needy state. Justice needs to burn deeply in the hearts of the people who reach out to others, so that they do not look at their efforts as *charity* or *good works*, but rather as that to which people have a God-given right. Good education, proper healthcare, safety in the home and on the streets, enough food, jobs for self-sufficiency, and the opportunity to be involved in achieving them—all are part of a just world, brought about by people who believe deeply and live justly and help others to do the same.

COLLABORATIVE

It is essential that efforts be collaborative. The best plans will fail if there is needless duplication that leads to a waste of money, time, and efforts. During the visit to the Canadian primary healthcare team mentioned above, I spent a day going with the sisters to visit other groups working in the same inner city area. On one hand, I was inspired by the number of people who were interested and committed enough to try to make a difference. On the other hand, however, as I told the sisters at the end of the day, I was distressed that there was not more collaboration among the groups, because they were duplicating, needlessly, many of the same efforts in such areas as accessing funds, deploying staff, and publicizing the need. Fortunately, they were not competing.

The most basic collaboration is between those who are trying to help and those needing the help. This precedes and is essential to any successful effort. The second level is collaboration among programs or groups involved in the same community, or in similar efforts. It is important to recognize the natural segments of a community and take an integrated stance. Depending on the circumstances, there can be multiple approaches to collaboration. Thus, in a neighborhood it is important to involve the schools, the churches, the businesses, the police, and any other recognizable groups in what is being attempted. A parish food bank or cupboard can be helped by approaching some of the neighborhood stores for donations or for help in getting what is needed.

In our neighborhood we spent several years organizing, block by block, a neighborhood street clean-up project, only to be frustrated by the local public grade school putting out its trash on Saturday night when pick up was not until Monday morning. Since the trash included boxes used in the school lunch program, the plastic trash bags attracted dogs and cats who ripped the bags open. After many of us complained about it, one neighbor who volunteered in the school brought it to the attention of the school principal. It was such a simple solution that we were embarrassed not to have thought of it sooner.

Major problems require collaboration on a larger scale. If we are trying to do something to help teenagers, we need to involve families, schools, churches, the police, and businesses in the area. Without collaboration we run the risk of duplication, but worse, we risk having some of the efforts negated by those not involved in the solutions.

Many of the programs being run by healthcare systems depend on the involvement of other institutions or groups in an area. Most important for many healthcare initiatives is the interaction with schools. If healthcare systems are to move toward outreach within neighborhoods, they need to collaborate with neighborhood organizations such as community councils. This is to ensure the involvement, not only of the people to be served, but also of the people in whose area the outreach will take place. Otherwise the "not in my neighborhood" syndrome can occur.

Schools attempting new approaches to children with problems know they need to involve parents. However, they often overlook other potential collaborators, such as the local churches which may have a strong interest in the same population. A group most frequently overlooked in neighborhood efforts are senior citizens. We have done a good job, in one sense, of providing more financial security for our seniors, but often we fail to pay attention to the rich resource they themselves are for the broader community. Programs that build in seniors help both the children and the older people at the same time. Not all senior citizens want to spend their remaining years of life centered on themselves and their leisure. What makes life rich is the knowledge that you are helping to make a difference for others. Now even nursing homes are providing ways for their residents to interact in a helpful way with children, or with other seniors in the area through shared programs.

The corporate world has collaborative potential that needs to be tapped. In a number of cities, public and private school systems are making connections with large companies to get assistance. Thus, companies may adopt a school, or commit to helping a school meet a particular need. Poorer schools, in both the public and private systems, often have difficulty getting the necessary equipment to provide for their students. Recently, I saw in a national paper an ad telling of poor schools in need of computers and asking if companies that were upgrading their equipment would consider donating usable equipment. Often all that is needed is a direct approach to a company. At the same time, many corporations, for varied reasons, see the value of encouraging community service for their employees, but have to search out potential sites. The dialogue has to be two-way for success.

Universities, especially those that are in or adjacent to inner city neighborhoods, can also be invited to collaborate. A principal of a parish school was asked by a nearby university if student teachers could be placed in the school. She responded positively, but asked that there be a commitment on the part of the university to helping the school with some after-school programs in the arts and in sports. The university was glad to collaborate and a number of students who were not student teachers were interested. High school and college students often want to participate in community-based projects, but don't know how to go about it unless the schools offers guidance. Collaboration provides a twofold advantage, both in terms of the communities helped and the students whose social awareness is developed. Some of the students are changed for life by their experiences.

Collaboration with government often seems impossible for people to even envision, and yet there are a number of programs around the country where it is taking place. Most frequently, and in fact appropriately, the collaboration is at the city level. It is appropriate because the closer the government is to the people, the more likely it is that what is being designed will work. Cities are especially likely to be collaborative with healthcare and educational initiatives, but are also interested in neighborhood projects. The city of Philadelphia has worked for many years through an organization of neighborhood organizations. This group keeps the city administration in touch with the various neighborhoods in a way that is different from the connection based on city services such as trash collection, water, police, and social services. Often cities are able to provide expert advice, agency services, and even, on occasion, funds. With the passage of the 1996 welfare reform bill, the movement of federal money via block grants to states is causing many cities to seek ways of accessing money for the needs of their communities.

The greater the levels of collaboration, and the more groups that do the collaborating, the greater will be the effect.

Money will be saved by avoiding duplication, and that money then can be directed to other needs. Another very wonderful effect is the sense of the strength in numbers that people get when more than one group or institution is involved with the same need or program.

"SMALL IS BEAUTIFUL"

What is very typical of many of the successful programs described earlier in the book is that they tend to be small and relatively simple. This does not prevent them from being both sophisticated and effective. What is important is that the best programs are those most in touch with the people and the community. In all the discussion of welfare reform over the past several years, one thing became very clear, and that was the wastefulness of large-scale bureaucracy, whether federal, state, or local. The discovery that 80 percent of the funds for welfare were used for overhead, e.g., salaries for workers, while only 20 percent went to those people on welfare was mind-boggling. One had to wonder who the real welfare recipients were! In addition to the financial waste, there is also the fact that those working in the bureaucratized welfare services have little contact with the actual people in need. Not only the politicians but also administrators can distance themselves from the reality.

In many parts of the Two-Thirds World there has been a growing awareness of the importance of using appropriate technology. This means that if a simpler approach will work, that is the approach that should be used; there is no need to invest in more sophisticated and expensive technology. Not only does this save money, but it also keeps the operation in the hands of those who need to be involved. A neighborhood breakfast program for children in Lima, Peru, is run by the women of the barrio, using the foods that are available locally and prepared in the usual way. Large pots, people doing the stirring, children bringing their own bowls... it works because it is possible. Prepackaged foods and microwave ovens would make no sense here given the poverty and the lack of electricity. This approach is inexpensive, since it uses readily available and traditional foods, and it is appropriate, since it involves the women of the barrio. Eventually, the same women started their own bakery. They built their own simple structure with seconds from the brick factory, contracted for the necessary masons and carpenters, and soon had their own small bakery. There a baker with two assistants makes 5,000 additive-free whole-grain rolls that are served to the children each morning with their vegetable stew. This very simple bakery and the equally simple kitchen is providing a healthy meal for the children of the neighborhood and employment for three bakers.

The Western world has an endless fascination with technology and with elaborate and large systems. For some things this is necessary, but one has to be sure that it really is necessary and that it improves the outcome. Simplicity is often the central element of programs that work. It makes the program doable, and often less expensive. For example, some healthcare delivery programs operate out of vans that travel through neighborhoods. In one compact unit they can carry everything necessary to meet most of the health needs they will encounter.

A similar approach is the use of a single room in a local school or in the basement of a church, or in a storefront clinic. The question to be asked is: What will most encourage involvement and use by the people? In one city, a supermarket chain has been providing community health services, such as blood pressure readings and cholesterol testing, in a room set aside for that on a daily basis. While one might be suspicious of the company's motive, it is providing good services in a relatively poor area and doing this quite simply in a place where people go regularly.

Simplicity requires clarity of vision and the ability to make distinctions. For example, it is important to distinguish between the obligations of a government, which are helpful and necessary, and the workings of its bureaucracy, which may be neither. If the bureaucracy is using up a disproportionate percentage of the available funding without showing significant value, it needs to be challenged. The further the service is from the people to be helped, the more likely it is that it needs simplification.

LEVELS OF RESPONSIBILITY DEFINED

Strategies that work have clear definitions of responsibility. Where there is a pattern of overlapping or unclear lines of responsibility there is also a lack of clear functioning. Government programs are often problematic because they fail to clearly delineate who is responsible for what. Responsibility entails accountability, and in any good program people must know for what they are responsible and to whom they are accountable.

The first group for whom any program and its people are responsible is the group served. More often than we would like to admit, this is a completely missing level of accountability. Adding to the problem, programs at times have different groups for which they are responsible. In a well-integrated program, everyone involved has clear accountability. When I was quietly sitting in that welfare office, watching what was going on, I wondered about responsibility to clients and about accountability. I speculated on how the rude or unhelpful behavior of some staff members could be challenged. Ideally, the ones to challenge such behavior would be the clients, but in such a setting the fear of reprisal runs too high. When I spoke with the social worker, I asked about this and her sad reply indicated that no one actually checked up on anything other than whether staff members were late or absent or took excessively long breaks. Not all welfare cheats are clients. While people often view responsibility and accountability as onerous, the fact is that when these are high and clearly defined, everything works more smoothly for all involved.

In any strategy there are different responsibilities. Some are delegated to staff, to professional people, to volunteers, to the people themselves. In community-based programs, accountability is best handled through a community board made up of members from the community serving and being responsible to the people themselves and to other groups that may be part of the collaboration. One community board on which I served was accountable, not only to the local people, but also to the national board of the church that was helping with funding. This made each of us on that board aware that in addition to being overseers of the handling of the funds by the director of the community center, we had a responsibility to stay clear and focused on our goals and the implementation of them.

REPLICABILITY

As I worked through the many different successful strategies used by groups and organizations, I came to realize how replicable they are. Good strategies can be tried by groups other than the ones who originated them. Thus, a program of housing assistance developed by one group frequently can be duplicated by another, with certain adaptations for place and population. Not everyone has to re-invent the wheel. Much of my regular reading is about things going on in Asia, Africa, and Latin America. While occasionally I do not see any direct application to the United States, it is usually because of the specificity of the target. Thus, an interesting approach to the prevention of sleeping sickness in Africa may not be open to direct replication in the United States or Europe. However, the *methods* used might be applicable in dealing with other health problems. The uses of vans in neighborhoods in this country to take healthcare to the people is not so different from medical teams going "on trek" in Africa, taking their skill and medicines to outlying villages.

One of the things I have tried to show in this book is the large number of Two-Thirds World strategies that can be adapted and used in this First-World country. The grandmothers of Washington, D.C., working with teenagers in pregnancy prevention and ante-natal care programs have similarities with the village health workers being trained in many Two-Thirds World countries. When reading about American programs I often find myself recalling programs in other parts of the world, especially in Africa and Asia. Illiterate grandmothers in the United States, like illiterate grandmothers in Africa, can be trained to have a role in health.

Hospitals in many African countries are located in the central area of a region and extend their services through the outreach of village health centers. Many of these are staffed by health workers whose training, while simple, is sufficient to diagnose the conditions that account for 90 percent of the health problems and to recognize the other 10 percent that need a doctor or a hospital. In America, many emergency rooms have become the "village health center" for neighborhoods, but use very highly trained staff for the 90 percent as well as the 10 percent. A child with a bad cold and respiratory infection can be treated by someone with less training than a doctor, but if the only place to get help is the emergency room of a nearby hospital, that is where the parent will go. Many health systems would do well to *replicate* the successful primary healthcare approaches of Africa and Asia.

Even simpler programs in the areas of education, development of self-esteem among children, conflict management, neighborhood cleanup, and anti-graffiti efforts have been developed and need only to be adapted to other settings. The most successful programs are often also the most replicable. Thus, the best approach can sometimes be to help people find the wheel that has already been invented and adapt it to fit their needs.

INTEGRATED PLANNING

All good programs involve planning. It may be the relatively simple planning of a block committee figuring out all the things that need to be done to pull off a block party. Or, it may be more complex. When programs connect with other programs or with other groups and organizations, the various groups are well served by integrated planning. What can be disconcerting about government programs, at all levels, is the lack of such integration. One agency may be either duplicating or unknowingly obstructing the work of another agency. The larger and more distant the agencies, the more likely that one of these two realities will affect the eventual outcome.

When the work that is being planned has a community base, it is easier to identify the groups and organizations that will be either impacted or involved in similar efforts. For example, in a neighborhood it is obvious that the schools, the churches, and the sports teams are all working with and for the same children. In terms of programming and scheduling, an integrated planning approach will make better use of limited resources and eliminate timing conflicts. A number of the strategies described in this book have just such integrated planning built into them. The Mercy Mobile Health involves a health system, a city, and a pharmaceutical company. By planning together they can have one program instead of three, or they can have three programs in three different parts of the city working together rather than competing.

Integrated planning also helps everyone be more aware of the impacts of various programs and the decisions that need to be made at various levels. Sometimes separate neighborhood groups schedule different programs for the same time, thus reducing the number of potential participants. Celebrations of the multi-ethnic nature of the place where I live are successful because the Community Council and the Businesspersons Association meet regularly to discuss what will help to bring the neighbors together. Each group runs separate days, one a Super Sunday, and the other a Cultural Diversity Day. Separate dates are chosen, but both groups collaborate in planning and implementing for both celebrations and in accessing city services such as outdoor stages, lighting, and loudspeaker systems.

The same kind of integrated planning is needed in budgeting for programs that reach out to people in a community or in a city. As money becomes tighter, it becomes more important for community groups to work together to obtain maximum value from the funds available. Collaboration and integrated planning go hand in hand, leading to successful results and providing an important lesson in our very competitive world.

EDUCATIONAL COMPONENT

Most successful strategies incorporate a strong educational component. This can mean educating the community in ways to approach their needs, and educating professionals in ways to understand and adapt to different cultural or ethnic groups. Many of the strategies for dealing with at-risk children, especially in terms of conflict resolution, drugs, crime, and truancy, are connected with education for teachers, for parents, and for the involved institutions such as schools and hospitals.

Education of the public is also important. In the early 1980s when the country became aware of the realities of HIV and AIDS, a major educational effort was mounted by many groups to offset false information and to cut down on the scapegoating of homosexuals. Further efforts in education became essential when it became clear that the epidemic was not limited to that one population. More than anything else, education has probably been the principal factor in the slowing of the epidemic in this country. The lack of education in some parts of the world, especially parts of Africa, has led to nationwide epidemics of horrendous size.

Whether a program is developed to help people access healthcare, start in-home work projects, organize neighbors to resist the incursion of drugs or clean up the streets, the first step is education. At one point, when the people on our street were having considerable difficulty with a group of angry teenage boys, we called on a woman from the city's social service community who was known to be an expert in gangs. She spent an hour with a half-dozen women and gave us enough information so that, by the end of the summer, we had a good handle on what had threatened to become a major problem, especially for some of our elderly.

Every community and every neighborhood has available a whole corps of professionals who can be accessed for help. We find them in the local schools, hospitals, police precincts, and social service agencies. As citizens, we can call on them for help. We are gradually finding other sources within our own neighborhoods and among local businesses. We discovered our own private gardening expert in a woman who lives on our street and had for years been a judge at the Philadelphia Flower Show, the premier show of its kind. Now retired, she found a whole new interest in helping neighbors with their small gardens, and the children with their gardening in barrels. She also rediscovered what it was like to be needed and appreciated beyond her small family.

It is also necessary to consciously educate some of the local institutions about their roles in the community. Schools, churches, businesses of all kinds can be helped to see that they have something to offer beyond their immediate and ordinary services. When I was an eighth grader in a parish school, we had a series of talks through the year from people in the parish who worked in different fields. We heard the local doctor, lawyer, and undertaker as well as teachers and business-people. They talked about the work they did, the training they needed, and how, as we moved on to high school, we should start planning for what we might want to do with our lives.

What was most engaging about their talks was the broadening of our horizons beyond the work our parents—mostly our fathers—did. Many of us had never before realized that we were not limited to what our families did, nor were we bound by gender. When some of the boys asked why the girls were at the talk given by the doctor, he made it clear that there was a future in medicine for women. Since there were no women doctors in our neighborhood, this was a learning experience for many of the eighth graders.

For the poor in our country, education in its broader sense is increasingly necessary. Our neighbor who started her own in-home day care center had to learn about how to prepare, how to get licensed, and eventually how to fill out small business tax forms. Much of this education is being facilitated not only by cities, but also by churches and public schools. High schools that were open only at night for school sports or senior plays, now run programs from computer literacy to how to play bridge or do Tai Chi.

In our increasingly diverse country, many parishes and community centers are sponsoring programs that teach English as a second language and offer courses in adult literacy and G.E.D. preparation. Education has both stayed in and moved beyond the school; it has also moved beyond the traditional-age student. As these changes are taking place, community is being strengthened on all sides.

CHAPTER 11

Who Is Responsible and How?

"When you give a feast, invite the poor, the maimed, the lame, the blind, and you will be blessed, because they cannot repay you. You will be repaid at the resurrection of the just."
(Luke 14:14)

We come back, finally, to the reality of the compassionate community which lives justly and therefore is concerned about the poor, the sick, the homeless, those suffering violence. This book has chronicled the sources for some of the poverty in our present world and has called attention to programs and strategies that have been developed by caring people in many walks of life. We must take hold of the notion that the good of the people, all of the people, is the responsibility of all of the people, individually and communally, locally and nationally, privately and publicly. There are many different roles that are appropriate, but all depend on a value base that recognizes that all people are worthy of respect, that we are responsible for ourselves and for one another. Without such recognition, a society can devolve to the lean and mean of the most brutish of levels where competition and warfare among and between are the norm.

What is growing clearer as we move through the last years of this century is that the paradigm of rugged individualism is being supplanted by a rediscovery of the spiritual base of life. Whether that spirituality is found in the traditional religions of Judaism, Christianity, Islam, Buddhism or in the humanism of

New Age thinking and the holistic movement, there is a clear reality emerging. People are looking for deeper meaning in their own lives and are finding it in a renewed sense of community. The spirit that is moving among so many is often challenged by the powers of darkness, the powers of self-centeredness associated with the "me" generation, the powers of self-serving at the cost of others.

Between 1994 and 1997 the U.S. Congress has promoted an ethic of taking care of yourself and your own. It has succeeded in cutting back on assistance to the neediest by appealing to the need to take care of our children. There is a strong, if somewhat subtle, suggestion that by "our children" is meant "our biological children." In reality, society's children are *all the children*, and the future of the society is based on all the children. While there are some people who accept the philosophy being preached in the halls of Congress, there are many others who are appalled by it. They find it unacceptable to give tax breaks to the wealthy, to corporations, and to pay for it out of school lunch programs, Medicaid, and AFDC.

For any country to be worthy of itself and its people, it has to have a broader understanding of the responsibilities that all have for all. It needs a compelling vision that links the future of the society with the care of and for the whole community of people who make it up. In the growing search for spirituality in our age, there is an emerging vision of a better and more compassionate and just community. The book of Proverbs (29:18) reminds us that where there is no vision the people perish. The leaders of the emerging future will be, undoubtedly, the ordinary people who make up our neighborhoods, cities, and countries. However, these ordinary people will have an extraordinary sense of commitment. They will be those who see the concern for others as a normal part of life and of the human journey.

ROLES IN THE NEW SOCIETY

In the coming years, in the third millennium, it will be important to reconsider the many people, groups, organizations, and parts of government which will need to be involved to bring about a compassionate society which cares for all its members. The roles that are necessary to move from where we are to where we would like to be are diverse. There is a place for everyone.

Personal and Community Roles

Responsibility begins with the individual. To say that others should help does not negate the basic reality that the person in need is called upon to do what is possible in terms of self-help. To call upon others is not to deny personal responsibility, but rather to accept the fact that at times people need help. The angry teenager who is truant and creating havoc in the neighborhood can theoretically stop the behavior and change. An intervention may be essential. Family, teachers, religious leaders, or even other teenagers may have to help the offender understand the anger and shift its focus. Schools and churches often miss opportunities to make the intervention that will help, perhaps even save, this teenager.

Families, especially in their extended form, have responsibility for one another in a very fundamental way. The parent whose response to teenage misbehavior is to simply shrug it off (commenting, as I heard one neighbor say, "They just have to be teenagers") is denying her own responsibility and that of the children. However, not every individual has had the advantages and role models to learn how to be a good parent. In most states it is harder to get a driver's license than to get a marriage license, and no license is required to bring a child into the world.

The local community has a responsibility to the individual or family in trouble. In a large city this may be a neighborhood, a block, a local church or social group. In some cases, it is the local school which may be the first to recognize a need. In all of these groups, the reaching out may be done by the group or by a single concerned person. Many city neighborhoods have developed ways for neighbors to help neighbors, and for neighbors to unite to change dangerous or unhealthy situations. We see and hear of people taking back their streets from drug pushers, or working with one another to provide greater safety from crime through town and block watches. Neighbors also help one another to beautify the space in which they live through block cleaning, urban gardening, and painting over graffiti-defaced walls.

Communities taking care of their own people is a next step in the process, but it is essential that there also be a community of communities which can be a source of encouragement, of challenge, and of assistance to individual communities whose problems are beyond what they can handle alone. Many of the programs that work are local endeavors that involve the collaboration of various communities to achieve common ends.

Government Roles

Over the past decade there has been much disagreement about the role of government in the areas of human services, welfare, healthcare reform, and education. What is key to a true understanding of government in any country is the fact that the *government is at the service of the people.* Government is for the people and has to keep the good of the people as central, both in terms of political and social issues. This does not mean that the government has to do everything for its citizens. That which people can do for themselves they should do for themselves. What has decayed over the generations, and very strongly so in the last half of this century, is the connection of the people to the various power groups.

While I dislike having to agree with anything held by the supply side theorists and the political proponents of the lean and mean approach, I do believe that big government is not necessarily the best way to serve the needs of the people. There has been growth in governmental bureaucracies over the last fifty years. While this is partly connected to the growth of the country and its needs, it is also related simply to government's ability to grow at a very fast pace. I am not at all convinced that all government bureaucracies are either needed or productive. One thing these bureaucracies do well is to provide employment for many people, but one has to wonder how efficient and effective these large groups are. Thus, I do not advocate continual growth of the governmental bureaucracies that have fed on the poor and vulnerable even while helping them.

Government, at different levels, has a number of key roles that only it can play. If it does not do so, then it needs to be questioned in terms of its very right to govern and its reason for being. Government is not established to care for those who govern.

Identification of Areas of Concern: A primary role of government is the analysis of areas of concern. This involves identifying incentives for action, sometimes helping to bring together the various social sectors, and providing some of the financial power. Some areas of concern, such as the environment, are of such magnitude that only the federal government can make the determinations of what is necessary. Other areas of concern may be the appropriate domain of states, counties, or cities.

Major Goal Establishment: At every level of government, with input from the people, governing bodies must set clear goals for the good of the people and the country. At the federal or central government level these would be broad national goals. Having set these goals, the government allots funding from the tax base to achieve them. It may be more efficient to use state, county, city, and local programs rather than national programs to achieve their goals. Standards and norms should be established both for initial distribution and continuation of funding.

Restructuring of Priorities in Spending: The federal government's discretionary spending for 1997 allocates $27 billion to the military. This is the highest item in the budget and consumes 53 percent of the spending—or $8,000 per second. Everything else, health, education, environment, crime fighting, drug interdiction, welfare, transportation, research, and so on, must compete somehow for the remaining 47 percent. Good budgeting in any organization needs to be connected to goals. Given these figures, our national goals are clearly more militaristic than social or even economic. Government at all levels needs to put the income from taxes to the effective accomplishment of the goals that best serve the good of all the people. Were the people to be heard in terms of what *they* believe is important, further growth of the military would probably not be as high on the list of priorities.

Tax Reform: During political campaigns in recent years the focus has usually been on tax reform, but much of the rhetoric has centered on tax reduction, with the greatest benefits going to the upper middle class and the rich. The emphasis has consistently been on reducing the taxes of the wealthy and large corporations. As a result, the middle class and the working class now pay an inordinate share of the taxes while many corporations with huge profits and wealthy individuals with smart tax lawyers pay less than their fair share. The tax restructuring that is needed is one that is based on *fairness,* one that recognizes that each should pay some share of the costs of the whole, but that those who have benefited the most should share the most. Such a tax restructuring should allow for control of the unjust gains made by some companies that benefit excessively from consumers or their own employees. A major needed change is to stop rewarding companies that enrich themselves by moving their factories off shore and then get a second reward in the area of tax breaks.

Comprehensive Family Policy: We hear politicians talking constantly about the centrality of the family and about family values, and yet there is a movement away from helping families to live those values. What is needed is some form of comprehensive family policy that guarantees minimal standards of care for every child, universal healthcare, nutritional and childcare subsidies, preschool programs for children who are at risk, and after-school programs for the children of working parents. National policy setting should be connected to state and local governments that establish programs to meet the needs of their people and communities. Federal funding should be commensurate with the types of programs and the number of people served. National standards would be one way of ensuring that people are aided in an equitable manner, regardless of where they live.

Assistance to Other Agencies: Government, whether at the federal, state, or local level, does not seem to be the best implementer of social programs. The movement of programs such as welfare from the federal to the state level may simply replace one large bureaucracy with fifty smaller ones. Like many foundations, government could establish clear goals and standards and then channel funds through non-governmental and non-profit groups which have demonstrated the ability to help those who are in need. Many agencies and church groups have shown that they can use funds very wisely. The closer they are to the communities and people in need, the better the funds are used. Most of these agencies do their work without setting up large and unwieldy staffs who seem accountable to no one, as is the case in so many government agencies. In the years when the United States was heavily involved in large-scale development programs in Two-Thirds World countries, it was not unusual for funds to be distributed through churches and missionaries who could be counted on to see that the funds got to the intended recipients rather than into the pockets of the politicians.

Major non-profit charitable agencies have a much better track record than government in terms of the ratio between money spent on overhead and that spent on programs. The recurring figure in terms of welfare is that 80 percent of the money goes into overhead, with only 20 percent going to the actual recipients. In its 1995 rating of the top five charities in terms of the most efficient use of money, the *NonProfit Times* listed the American Red Cross first, with 91.5 percent of its income going to programs. The other four, in order, were Catholic Charities USA with 87.7 percent on programs, the Salvation Army with 85.8 percent, Campus Crusade for Christ at 83.9 percent, and YWCA at 83.8 percent. Government might do well to consider these figures.

Churches and Religious Bodies

Throughout the history of the world, religious people and groups have played a truly prophetic role. Each of the great religions has a strong history of being on the side of the needy. Islam's emphasis on the virtue of hospitality was born out of its desert origins, since to fail in hospitality would be to condemn the stranger to serious distress and possible death. The Judeo-Christian call to care for the poor, the widow, children, and the stranger is something many people hear regu-

larly in the ritual readings in synagogues and churches. It is always distressing to find groups that call themselves religious
acting against the poor or the suffering, especially when they
do it in the name of religion.

Religions are organizationally committed to outreach.
Four of the five charities mentioned above have directly religious origins and ongoing connections. Their major sources
for funds are religious people who see contributing to these
charities as a way of carrying out a religious obligation. There
are a variety of ways in which religious organizations can facilitate the kind of change needed so badly.

Challenge to the People: It is easy for us to become so concerned about ourselves and our own families that we forget
those who have even less than we. Regularly, the churches remind us that our religious obligations extend beyond attend-
ing religious services. With the passage of the welfare reform
bill, the demands on non-governmental sources of funds will
increase. Part of the task of religious leaders will be to make
the needs of the poor and the obligations of all to be of help
major priorities in the coming years.

Calling for a just society is primarily a task of the churches. This includes preaching the inherent worth of the poor;
safeguarding the family; requiring fairness in the workplace
so that the workers are not penalized with reduced salaries
and benefits while top executives receive excessive salaries.
Historically, churches have played an important role in safeguarding the people of God. They now face a new challenge
in which they can add their voices and service to the public
debate.

Modeling Care and Concern: The religious community itself
can make an impact. People, individually and in groups, within the family and at the workplace, must be continuously challenged to take seriously the religious commitment which they
have made. In answer to the young man who had asked, "Who
is my neighbor?" Jesus told the parable of the Good Samaritan, the one who saw the man beaten and left on the roadside
and took care of him. People who consider themselves "good"
Christians, or Jews, or Muslims...need to take to heart the
deeper challenges to living their beliefs.

There are many ways to carry out religious obligations: giving money, giving time, voting for socially just legislation, lobbying at all levels for a just and fair society for all, involving oneself in specific projects and programs. A number of churches include community service as part of the parish commitment. What one cannot do is walk away—as the priest and the Levite did in the parable—and still consider oneself religious.

Local religious communities can provide ways for people to become involved in their own neighborhoods or cities. Some churches have food pantries and run thrift shops. Many Catholic parishes now have social ministers who do direct service and also provide education, awareness, and training for people who want to become active. After the Million Man March of 1995, several churches in my neighborhood invited the men who had gone on the march to Washington to become involved in neighborhood efforts, including repairing a recreation center and cleaning up some dangerous empty lots. The neighborhood paper and local TV stations covered the response, focusing attention on and supporting the call of the churches to the men who had been touched by their Washington experience. Recently, a number of these men were honored for the way in which they have been trying to carry out their commitments during the year. The 1997 Million Women March in Philadelphia had representatives and support from the religious community, both in the city and among the many women who came to take part. The African-American women who took part were encouraged to look to their religious traditions as a lifespring in helping to create a more just world.

Local clergy need to be conscious of preaching the social message as part of the spiritual message. They have many opportunities to talk to their people about the demands of justice as *inherent* to a religious commitment. Each local church, synagogue, and mosque needs to be made aware of the global, the national, and the local calls for compassionate justice, and how it can be part of the effort, not a part of the problem.

Religious Congregations

In the Catholic Church, religious congregations of women and men have a strong prophetic basis. They challenge the world and the church itself to respond to newly emerging needs which are not being met and to suffering which has not been succored. From the earliest days of the first-century Christian community until the present religious women and men have followed as best they could the call of the Beatitudes. Over the ages their methods have changed, but their purpose has remained the same. In the nineteenth century many religious women's congregations became involved in education and healthcare and developing large systems of hospitals and schools. At the end of the twentieth century they are turning these institutions over to educated and dedicated lay people, and are moving into the alternative approaches called for in the present age. While being involved in these alternative approaches themselves, they are continually bringing the laity into and involving them in these same works. Often it is the religious congregations that have the knowledge and the courage to step out into the new and provide a place for lay volunteers on a full- or part-time basis. Many of the successful strategies described in the earlier chapters of this book are connected to religious congregations, often started by them, and at times funded by them.

Religious today can be found in many different places: serving the poor in homeless shelters and public health clinics; driving around the inner city in a health van; marching for renters' rights in inner city neighborhoods; lobbying at the state capitol and on Capitol Hill in Washington; holding vigil and praying at prisons in opposition to the death penalty, which is usually imposed for crimes committed by the poor and minorities. Religious in the twenty-first century may be fewer and less immediately recognizable, but they will be working *as they have always worked* to hear the cries of the poor and respond. They will continue their educational and healing roles, doing so in a greater variety of places and styles, committed as they always have been to the prophetic demands of their calling.

Community Service Organizations

There are many institutions in society which carry the name or the history of community service, in the sense that their reason for being is to be of service to a community. The main service organizations are the schools, law enforcement agencies, healthcare systems, and social service agencies. In some cases there is a need to recapture the meaning of service or to make a recommitment to it. For some of these groups, the schools and healthcare systems, the move in the direction of for-profit business is a threat to the true nature of service to children or to the sick. In law enforcement, the danger lies more in the perception among the police that they are at war against instead of in service to those most in need. Even the language used, "the war on crime" or "the war on drugs," can subtly lead into an adversarial stance. Many social service agencies have become so enmeshed in the bureaucracy and in the questionable professionalization of roles that the simple call to be of service has become blurred.

All of these service organizations need to rediscover the source of their power and their value. They must be willing to move more creatively into the future in a mode which focuses on working with those in need, whether in education, healthcare, protection, or development.

Private Sector

This last half century has seen a huge growth of large corporations and multinationals. Very often these organizations have profit as their prime goal, so that the good of the workers and their families must be safeguarded by unions and by government regulations. The further management moves from its workers, the easier it is to engage in practices that are harmful to those who actually produce the profits.

There are important roles that corporations can and should play without being forced to do so by government. Corporate leaders do not exist in a vacuum. They too have roots in a religious tradition and a social reality which should lead them to a re-examination of their philosophy of business and its impact on workers, on consumers, on the world at large.

Every corporation has obligations to employees for decent wages, benefits, training, and termination assistance when downsizing is inevitable. Companies should look hard at the enormous gap between CEO and management salaries and those of the workers and voluntarily make just changes. It seems unjustifiable that a CEO should receive millions of dollars in salary when workers are at minimum wage and unable to care for their families, even though they work hard. Profit sharing is a way of leveling the field between management and workers, a way of recognizing that all collaborate in producing the company's profit.

Companies often benefit directly from the communities in which they are located. They benefit through tax incentives, a school system which prepares their future employees, and a whole network of services related to utilities, transportation, and other supportive benefits. In return, they need to give back direct service to these communities. Companies can contribute to communities by providing materials, services, and expertise to community programs and institutions. Corporations that are socially inert become parasites, justifying their existence by saying that they provide jobs, while in fact they take much more from the community than they give back.

Foundations

Through establishing a foundation, a large national or multinational corporation can channel some of the profits back to the people who helped produce those profits, or to those who have been harmed by the actions of the company. Whether the large and multi-faceted, or small and tightly focused, foundations have been a way for the corporations to pay their debt to the society that helped to make them successful. During this century foundations have been significantly involved in supporting institutions of higher education and large-scale healthcare endeavors.

What is needed increasingly as well is the funding of those relatively small, community-based projects that have the potential to become models for change. The U.S. Catholic Bishops' foundation, The Campaign for Human Development, has provided seed money for many self-supporting cooperative projects that provide education and skill development so that people can break the cycle of dependency. The Robert Wood Johnson Foundation has made a commitment to help bring about changes in the healthcare system. Its initial emphasis on primary healthcare projects has had a significant impact on small local community health centers. The Connelly Foundation has been funding inner city Catholic schools that are successful in their work with children in poverty. The funds provide for further in-service training for the teachers as well as high school scholarships for the students.

All People of Good Will

Many of the people who have been involved in the projects described in this book, as well as many other projects, are ordinary, caring people who believe in living their values, and especially their religious commitment. Many of these projects would not even have started had there not been women and men, and also children, who decided they had to do something. That something may be as simple as collecting cans of food for the local food pantry, or Boy Scouts picking up grapefruit and oranges in Florida neighborhoods to take to the Free Clinic in St. Petersburg.

A major source of volunteers has been the pool of senior citizens who want to do more with their retirement years than play bingo and go on trips. What they need, most often, is a base out of which to work, though many individual seniors start up their own neighborhood projects.

Another pool of volunteers is that of the famous people who may be, for example, sports stars, musicians, or actors and actresses. They are famous because of a public which has identified them, supported them, and often looked up to them. They too have an opportunity to give back. Some sports celebrities fund projects to teach their sport to inner city children, with the hope of keeping them in school, even if they never become professionals in the sports world. Some musicians have returned to their places of origin and given back to the community by helping to fund projects. Former President Jimmy Carter and former First Lady Rosalyn Carter provide a powerful example through their commitment to Habitat for Humanity. They do not simply give money, or lend their names, but they contribute their own time and energy in the actual rehabilitation of houses.

Professional people from all walks of life can be of direct assistance. They can offer their expertise or provide *pro bono* services to agencies, projects, and helping organizations. Children can be drawn into helping roles through their schools, churches, or families. A number of years ago Philadelphia was fascinated by Trevor, a young boy who, after watching the news about the homeless one night, decided he wanted to go downtown and give his pillow and blankets to a homeless man. From that small start grew a whole outreach project of assistance to homeless people sleeping on the city's streets. A little child can lead them.

CHAPTER 12

What Is the Future That We Want?

*"The community of believers devoted themselves
to the apostles' teaching and mutual sharing ...
awe and reverence came upon them all."*
(Acts 2:42-43)

When faced with the problems and dysfunctional reality that surround us, many people want to respond with flight. There are no simple or easy solutions to social problems. The past is the most tempting of escapes. We always remember things under a roseate glow. When we were growing up, things were simpler, safer, better. Yet when we examine the past more carefully, we find that there were problems then too. The past can be instructive for us. We can learn about things that worked and things that failed. What we cannot do is turn back the clock. We need to live in our own age and work out ways to make it possible to live more creatively and fully.

As we move toward the third millennium, many feelings, fears, hopes, and desires arise. The millennium has been associated in the past with predictions of catastrophe, of the end of the world, as well as with hopes for a new and better world. Many writings in the last few years of the nineteenth century focused on the wonders of the coming twentieth century. New inventions seemed to promise only good things and the good life. Little attention was paid to the signs, easier to see in retrospect, that the world of the twentieth century would experience the disasters of two world wars, a major as well as some minor depressions, the Cold War, and immense migrations of refugees fleeing terrible oppression.

There is nothing magic about the change from one century to another, not even from one millennium to the next. What might happen at such times is that a sense of hope and wonder, a burst of creativity can, if well channeled, help to move people forward. This is one of those times. The last decade of the twentieth century has not been one of boundless positive progress. In fact, the 1990s seem to have been characterized by a sense of hopelessness on many fronts.

The mid-century hope, that having won the war we were moving into a wonderful new life for everyone, was not fulfilled. After a brief period of growth in the 1950s, things began to get worse for many people rather than better. By the mid-1960s the president was declaring a "War on Poverty." Now, in the last decade of the century, we find ourselves blaming many people; the poor for being poor, teenage unmarried mothers, welfare cheats, illegal (and legal) immigrants, deadbeat fathers, gays and lesbians, the chronically unemployed or underemployed. Rather than placing blame, we need to go to the root causes of our problems, identify what has to change, and then encourage everyone to become involved in the solutions.

One of Franklin Delano Roosevelt's greatest contributions was the realization that there is a time when the only viable source of change is at the federal level. Today there is a growing gap between those who are wealthy and those who are poor, between those who have hope for the future and those who are dying of despair. Since federal initiatives are not working, perhaps it is time to look to other sources for solutions.

WHAT OF THE FUTURE?

If we know anything, we know that what is happening now cannot continue. The world and its people have cycled many times through good and bad times, through good and bad ideas. Not too many years ago, I would find myself thinking, "come the revolution...things will change." That was before the revolution in Nicaragua was undermined by the actions of the United States and its military, and before the new revolution in Russia led to the embracing of a Western-style capitalism with all of its failings. I still believe that there can be a revolution, though it does not have to be one which is violent or military.

We need a revolution in commitment, in creativity, in caring if we are to change what seems to be an ever downward spiral. We have the ingredients for a better life for all. We have many different and successful approaches to the problems which plague our society and our world. What is necessary is the *will* to go in a different direction, to try something that involves government without depending upon it exclusively. It is not enough to eliminate government and then turn to charitable organizations, or to local communities, or to philanthropists... or to the private sector. We need to look at how *all* groups, peoples, and organizations can move in a collaborative way to make a new and different world as we move into the next millennium and beyond.

The world in which we live and function is the responsibility of all of us. Just as, in the words of the African proverb, it takes a whole village to raise a child, so too it takes a whole world to make a better life for everyone.

In the final analysis, the most successful approaches have always been the holistic ones. In the 1960s John F. Kennedy voiced the challenge of putting a man on the moon. The response to that challenge was probably one of the most collaborative efforts ever undertaken by any government. Watching that man walking on the moon, many of us wondered why other things could not be done as well. At the time of the moon walk I met a man who worked for NASA. Taking the "just back in the country" stance of a returned missionary, I asked him why it was that we could put a man on the moon, but could not produce low-income housing. I have never forgotten his answer. He told me that both efforts took three things: technology, money, and commitment. For the moon, all three were in place. There was technology, money, and commitment. For low-income housing, the technology is available, and money can be gotten, but, he said, "There is no commitment to low-income housing because it is not politically worthwhile." He may have been right or wrong, but it made sad sense to me.

To make a difference in the coming millennium, we need—to borrow this man's insights—three things. First, we need technology in the sense that we need to know what is required and how to develop it. Second, we need money, or the wherewithal to do what must be done. Third, we need the commitment, the will to make a difference. I believe the technology is already there, in the minds, in the books, in the studies that have been done, and in the successful strategies being used in many places. The money is also there, but perhaps not so available yet because it is being used for other things such as military hardware. The commitment, the will to make a difference, is what is most needed and what is most lacking.

Many people have the will and the desire to change the kind of world we live in. Many of them have access to the technology that is needed. Money is never a problem once you have the technology and the will. It is a matter of pulling together to make a different world for ourselves and others in the coming millennium.

This book has dealt with different approaches to the problems that we have as a society and as a world. There are failed strategies which, for some strange reason, we keep trying even when we know that they have failed. However, there are also highly successful strategies, ones that in fact do work, and which can be effectively applied. These are not simply theoretical models, but *actual programs and projects* that people are using to make a difference in their world. Many are small, and all can be replicated. Most need relatively little money; some require more funds. We have the money, individually and globally, for what we are committed to. We need to develop the commitment, and then we will find that we can make the difference, we can work on solutions that are just and compassionate, and we can build the community of the peoples of the world. We need to believe that we can do it, and then set about the work.

NEW WORLD ORDER

The challenge is to help in creating a new world order. This would be one in which major ills—such as unnecessary illnesses, hunger, poverty, homelessness, crime, and the despair of whole populations—are reduced, if not eliminated. The good life as a possible goal for all would be one well worth working to accomplish. What we do not want to do is to go into the twenty-first century with a growing divide, with a small segment at the top that has an unfair, unjust, and out-of-proportion piece of the pie while more and more people slip into poverty. The new world order will do more than help only the poor and the disenfranchised. *All* people will benefit from a society that functions more justly.

Such a society would experience a major reduction in crime achieved through the improvement of the lives of the people who suffer from poverty, lack of jobs, and poor education. It would cease wasting the rich and wonderful potential of children. Such a society would work to achieve better systems where the needs of all are cared for, where there are better schools, better civic government, safer cities, a healthcare system that works for all the people. While there will always be some crime, a new social order could eliminate the two most destructive forms of crime: it would eliminate the now mainly unpunished corporate crime that creates more problems than solutions, and it would reduce the crime that emerges at the other end of society from the need, the fear, and the despair of those who have nothing.

The description of the early Christian church of Jerusalem could be the picture of a future world based on justice, compassion, and community. A society in which *"Those who believed were of one heart... there was not a needy person among them... distribution was made to each as any had need" (Acts 4:32-35).*

Let us create that community now.

EPILOGUE

Jesus said to his followers: "When the Messiah comes in glory, together with all the angels, He will sit on on a glorious throne. All the nations will be gathered before the throne, and the Holy One will separate them one from another as a shepherd separates the sheep from the goats, and will place the sheep on one side and the goats on the other. Then the Chosen One will say to some,

> *"Come, O blessed ones of God, inherit the realm prepared for you from the foundation of the world; for I was hungry and you gave me food, I was thirsty and you gave me drink, I was a stranger and you welcomed me, I was naked and you clothed me, I was sick and you visited me, I was in prison and you came to me."*

Then those who were chosen will answer,

> *"When did we see you hungry and feed you, or thirsty and give you drink? When did we see you a stranger and welcome you, or naked and clothe you? When did we see you sick or in prison and visit you?" And the Holy One will answer them, "Truly, I say to you, as you did it to one of the least of these, my sisters and brothers, you did it to me."*

Then, turning to the others, the Chosen One will say,

> *"Depart from me, you cursed, into the eternal fire prepared for Satan and Satan's angels; for I was hungry and you gave me no food, I was thirsty and you gave me no drink, I was a stranger and you did not welcome me, naked and you did not clothe me, sick and in prison and you did not visit me."*

Then they also will answer,

> *"When did we see you hungry or thirsty or a stranger or naked or sick or in prison, and did not minister to you?"*

Then the Holy One will answer them,
*   "Truly, I say to you, as you did not do it to one of the least of*
*   these, you did not do it to me."*

And they will go away into eternal punishment, but the righteous into
eternal life. (Mt 25:31-46)

SOURCE LIST

This is a sample of the many successful programs and strategies that are currently being used to reach out as a compassionate people to those in need. This source list can also be used by those who want to learn more about how to do similar things. It is organized under several headings, related to the major efforts of the groups or their target populations.

THE ELDERLY

Food for Friends
Philadelphia, Pennsylvania
This is a city-wide program that provides food to shut-in elderly. Volunteers prepare meals or cook extra servings when cooking for families. The program provides aluminum serving dishes. Other volunteer drivers take meals to the shut-ins on whatever schedule is good for the recipients. Some receive meals daily, others several times a week.

Holy Redeemer Visiting Nurse Agency Food Bank
Holy Redeemer Visiting Nurse Agency
Swainton, New Jersey
Contact: Sr. MaryAnne McDonagh, CSR, 609-465-2082
In addition to running a visiting nurse program, this agency distributes food to poor and fixed-income elderly in three counties in southern New Jersey. It has a full-service food bank, supported mainly by donations from local business and community members. Its primary clients are elderly, but it also assists single mothers with children living in poverty and families affected by job loss or illness.

Mercy Brown Bag Program
Mercy Retirement and Care Center
Oakland, California
Contact: Mary Francis Giammona, 510-534-8540, ext. 369
This group collects and distributes donated and purchased nutrition-

175

al food to 540 low-income elderly in Alameda County. It encourages seniors to help others; provides nutritional and consumer information, referrals, and personal enrichment education; and collects and distributes about 750,000 pounds of donated food/year.

Project ElderCare
Hospital of St. Raphael
New Haven, Connecticut
Contact: John Merritt, M.D., 203-789-3989
The program provides convenient access to medical care for underserved, inner-city elderly in New Haven and operates three clinics in local low-income public housing projects for seniors.

FINANCING

First Community Bank
Washington, D.C.
This is a new bank designed to serve low- and moderate-income neighborhoods in Washington, D.C. The bank works closely with local financial institutions to increase access and responsible use of credit and with community organizations to produce affordable housing and to encourage entrepreneurship among the poor. It makes commercial, real-estate, and consumer loans available in an area of the city which has not had access to capital markets.

Grameen Bank
Dhakka, Bangladesh
President: Mohammed Yunus
This Two-Thirds World bank has set an example by providing loans to the poor. Starting with very small amounts, women and men can borrow at very low interest in order to start small businesses or to build homes. The bank now has branches in half of the villages of Bangladesh. It has been a force in the development of micro-lending around the world.

The Banco Internacional de la Mujer, The International Women's Bank
Anthony, New Mexico
This bank opened in 1994. It is based on a similar project in Mexico and the women who run it were trained by the Mexican federation, FEMAP. The bank provides small loans at very low interest to women who want to start their own businesses. The loans start at

$100 and can gradually be increased as the borrowers demonstrate their ability to meet the low-interest payments and establish the small businesses.

FOUNDATIONS

Campaign for Human Development
U.S. Catholic Conference
3211 4th St., NE
Washington, D.C. 20017-1194,
Phone: 202-541-3210, fax 202-541-3329
This arm of the U.S. Catholic Bishops Conference distributed over $200 million dollars in the first twenty-six years of its existence. The grants have touched the lives of nearly half the poor people in the U.S. The emphasis is on small, local projects that move people toward self-sufficiency and independence. Many have been used to establish small, worker-owned businesses. Criteria for grants: projects a) must benefit a group with at least 50 percent of the people coming from a low-income community; b) members of the poverty group must have a dominant voice in the project; c) the project must conform to the moral teachings of the Catholic Church; d) the project should innovatively address the basic causes of poverty and effect institutional change; e) the project should contribute to a more integrated and mutually understanding society. Source of funding: major fund drive in local churches each year.

In addition to funding community projects, the Campaign for Human Development also supports major educational programs: *Target*, a program of intensive justice education related to the preferential option for the poor, now operating in thirty-five dioceses and involving both diocesan staff and parishioners; *Middle Income Process*, which uses a focused retreat experience to give middle-class U.S. Catholics an opportunity to reflect on Catholic social teachings on the poor and the causes of poverty and to make a commitment to personal action.

Children's Defense Fund
25 E Street, NW
Washington, D.C. 20001
From its initiation the focus of the Children's Defense Fund has been on the care and safety of children who are at risk in modern society. A major, if not *the* major, voice for the rights of children and the respon-

sibility of all people to be concerned for the welfare of children. Advocacy for children has been a hallmark of this group from its inception.

Duke Endowment
North Carolina
Established in 1924 by industrialist James Buchanan Duke, the Duke Endowment makes grants to universities, colleges, hospitals, children's homes, churches, and pastors in the Carolinas.

Robert Wood Johnson Foundation
Princeton, New Jersey
Since the early 1970s this foundation has provided grants to organizations across the country to equalize access to the healthcare system by reducing sociocultural barriers that impede access to urban healthcare systems. Respect for differences of language, neighborhood, community ties, and diverse cultures is considered as important to delivering high-quality care as the education of the provider and the quality of the services.

HEALTH

1. General Programs

Community Health Nurse Outreach Program
Archbishop's Commission on Community Health
St. Louis, Missouri
This program has placed a nurse in five of the eight Catholic Community Service Centers. The nurses perform assessments, provide health education and screening, facilitate access to health services, and participate in case management teams.

Inmed
45449 Severn Way, Suite 161
Sterling, Virginia 20166
Phone: 703-444-4477, fax 703-444-4471
This non-profit organization enables disadvantaged people worldwide to improve the health of families and communities. Since 1986 it has established community-based programs in ninety-three countries. It also works to achieve partnerships among public and private sector groups. In 1990 it initiated a decade-long Millennium conference series to bring together experts from around the world to share

on major steps in healthcare improvements world wide. The organization fosters many innovative programs.

Parish Health Ministry Nurse Program
Archbishop's Commission on Community Health
St. Louis, Missouri
This program helps parishes with initial health assessments, screenings, and education so that each parish can tailor its programs to its own needs. It has developed a how-to manual for starting a parish health ministry. In addition, it provides mentors and links hospitals with parishes for better integrated care.

St. Joseph's Mercy Care Mercy Mobile Health Care
Atlanta, Georgia
Established in 1994, this program has five vans and two medical units that deliver primary healthcare, social services, education to 17,000 people. It services twenty-nine shelters, clinics, and housing communities and has a forty-six unit residence for low-income individuals with HIV/AIDS. It collaborates with other community groups to focus on the special needs of women and children.

2. Mothers and Children

Foundation for Higher Education
Colombia, South America
The Foundation for Higher Education has trained voluntary health workers from the community to identify and treat common maternal and child health problems. Workers are assigned to fifty to sixty families in their own community. The program primarily uses mothers and grandmothers who visit families twice a month to provide health education and to update records.

Franciscan AIDS/Drug Baby Home
Philadelphia, Pennsylvania
Three Franciscan sisters act as legal foster parents to infants born to parents with AIDS or drug addictions. The health of these children is fragile and "Sr. Moms" care for them full time in a home setting. The home, which opened in 1990, cared for twenty-three children in its first five years. When, at around the age of two, children who test negative for HIV are medically stable, they are placed in pre-adoptive homes. The sisters remain in contact with the children during the transition time to the new home.

Head Start Program of Washington Heights
New York, New York
Washington Heights has a largely immigrant population. The program provides education and health and social services and emphasizes parental involvement. High-risk families are taught how to function as a unit. The program uses prevention and intervention models and encompasses lay involvement and community partnerships.

King-Drew Medical Center, Department of Pediatrics
Watts neighborhood
Los Angeles, California
The department trains personnel for ninety day care centers in the area and collaborates with the public school system through a magnet high school in health sciences on the grounds of the hospital.

St. Mary's Women and Infants Center
Caritas Christi
736 Cambridge St.
Boston, Massachusetts 02135
Contact: Joyce A. Murphy, President, 617-436-8600
A diocesan sponsored program to assist the Dorchester neighborhood, the center provides interdependent services, some funded by the health system and some by government or other sources. The area, which had the highest infant mortality rate in Boston, has a population which is 49 percent African-American, 32 percent white, 15 percent Hispanic, and 4 percent Asian. Twenty-five percent of the people are below the poverty line, and the median income is 35.5 percent below that of households nationwide. The center has developed a community program involving residents, city and church leaders, public and private health and social agencies. It provides residential and healthcare services for women and children, as well as education on parenting, health, and safety. A short-term residence service for children in the custody of the Department of Social Services provides counseling, recreation, and therapeutic services. One hundred twenty women and children are assisted every day. The center also provides comprehensive out-patient services including counseling and help for victims of domestic violence, in a neighborhood clinic.

School Health Partnership
St. Joseph's Care Group
South Bend, Indiana
Contact: Barbara Lohr, 219-237-6814

This is a school nurse program sponsored by St. Joseph's Medical Center of South Bend and St. Joseph Community Hospital of Mishawaka, Indiana. The hospitals train volunteer nurses to provide services to 6,000 students in twenty-one Catholic schools in the area. The schools recruit parents who are nurses to volunteer and the hospital coordinators help the volunteers learn how to provide vision, hearing, and scoliosis screening, report communicable diseases, document testing, and administer flu and hepatitis vaccinations. The emphasis is on preventive healthcare. This is a good example of collaboration between health systems, schools, and professionals (R.N.s).

Strong Beginnings
Columbia University
New York, New York
The university collaborates with Save the Children in a program for children up to age three that provides education in parent-child interactive learning with special emphasis on health and nutrition and family literacy. The program also provides day care.

3. Pregnant Women and Teenage Pregnancy

Community of Caring
Granite School District
Salt Lake City, Utah
Using the approach fostered by Eunice Kennedy Shriver, Community of Caring provides education programs for parents and teens. The goal is the prevention of teenage pregnancy. Based on a values program, it arranges for teens to talk with other teens who have been pregnant and had babies; the emphasis is on the reality—as opposed to the fantasy—of what it means to have a baby. This is a very successful prevention program.

Friends of Moms Program
Archbishop's Commission on Community Health
St. Louis, Missouri
Women are trained to identify unserved pregnant women in their neighborhoods and to get them early, continuous, and holistic antenatal care. Of the first sixty babies born in the program's first year none died and none were of low birth weight. The program demonstrates the importance of good ante-natal care and the value of involving other women in the community.

Health Beginnings Plus
Frankford Hospital
Frankford Ave. & Wakeling St.
Philadelphia, Pennsylvania 19124, 215-831-6790
This state-funded program of comprehensive ante-natal care for those on Medicaid is designed to reduce infant mortality. It provides one-on-one support throughout the pregnancy of teenagers, a high-risk group, plus education in parenting skills.

Healthy Moms
St. Mary's Hospital
Rochester, New York
This ante-natal program emphasizing prevention and early intervention for at-risk urban women includes free child care, hot lunches, transportation, and help with preparing for employment.

Maternal Assistance Program (MAP)
Holy Spirit Hospital
Camp Hill, Pennsylvania
Program Director: Joyce A. Zandieh, R.N.
Established to reduce the incidence of substance abuse in pregnant women and new mothers, this program creates a bridge between peri-natal and substance abuse services in the community. It focuses on case management, facilitating access to available community resources. Referrals are received from various healthcare providers, county courts, probation and parole offices, children and youth services. The clients, who are visited weekly in their homes, are helped to set goals and become self-reliant. The program also addresses problems with transportation and babysitting. In its second year (1994–95) the program served 91 clients and in 1995–96 it served 102.

MotherNet America: Inmed
This is one of the programs supported by Inmed. It provides a network for lay home visiting programs designed to reduce infant mortality and other risks facing pregnant women and families with young children. The network connects with clinics, churches, and schools and offers training for new mothers, which is especially important given the reduction of time spent in the hospital after delivery.

Project MotherCare
Hospital of St. Raphael
New Haven, Connecticut
New Haven is the seventh poorest city of its size in the U.S. In 1989 it

led the nation in infant mortality, with 18.5 deaths/1000 live births. The hospital turned a 58-foot tractor trailer into a clinic on wheels to bring ante-natal care to underserved neighborhoods. It also reached out to substance-abusing pregnant women by providing counseling, social services, and ear acupuncture as supportive therapy for drug abusers. Infant mortality at the hospital dropped from 17.1/1000 in 1990 to 6.25/1000 in 1993.

4. City/Community Programs and Collaborations

Clinica Guadalupana
Horizon City, Texas
This clinic, run by the Sisters of Charity of Cincinnati, was built with donations of money and services through a public-private collaboration between the clinic, the public health department, and the Sisters. It provides primary and preventive healthcare and also runs program TEAM (Together Everyone Achieves Miracles) to build self-esteem among teenage girls.

Community Mobilization for Health
Dhakka, Bangladesh
The aim is to reduce mortality and morbidity among children under age six and women ages fifteen to forty-five through immunizations, maternal care, nutrition education, and oral rehydration. It uses networking among public and private sectors and educates local leaders in managerial, technical, and fundraising skills. Emphasis is placed on community surveillance of preventable diseases and pneumonia. In the program's first year, 92.5 percent of the children were immunized; 82 percent of mothers learned correct infant feeding practices. This is a bottom-up community-based program that mobilizes all socioeconomic classes and develops neighborhood health committees.

Mercy Care Mobile Health
Mercy Health System
Philadelphia, Pennsylvania
Director: Gloria McNeil, 610-237-4895
This is a collaborative program involving Mercy Health Corporation, the City of Philadelphia's Partnership for Progress, and Smith-Kline Beecham, a pharmaceutical company. Started in 1996, it has the first mobile van that goes through underserved poverty areas to deliver primary and preventive healthcare to those with no insurance. The aim is to break down the financial, social, cultural, and

transportation barriers that prevent people from seeking proper healthcare and to fill the gap by linking people in need to available resources.

HOMELESSNESS

Christmas in April
Wharton School of Business & Orleans Technical Institute
Philadelphia, Pennsylvania
This is a program that involves students from both schools in rehabilitating houses. The students spend spring break working with groups that are rehabilitating houses for the homeless.

CommonBond Communities
Minneapolis, Minnesota
President: Joseph A. L. Errigo, Jr., of St. Paul.
This affiliate of the archdiocese of St. Paul and Minneapolis is the largest private, non-profit community development corporation in the U.S. Its emphasis is on low-income and elderly access to affordable housing. Since its founding in 1974, it has sponsored and now owns more than $70 million in housing, including 2,000 units in eighteen Minnesota communities.

Heartside Clinic
St. Mary's Health Services
Grand Rapids, Michigan
Contact: Anne Mawby, R.N., 616-774-6375
This storefront clinic provides primary and preventive healthcare for the homeless. It is the only provider of free medical and nursing care, social services, health education, mental health services, and substance abuse counseling in the area.

H.O.M.E. (Housing, Opportunities, Medical Care, Education)
1515 Fairmount Ave.
Philadelphia, Pennsylvania 19130
Phone: 215-232-7272
The stated mission of this group is "We commit ourselves to forming a Community of Hope, drawing its members from all walks of life, to respond to the needs of chronically homeless men and women of Philadelphia." It started with Women of Hope, a program for chronically mentally ill homeless women that provided living space,

food, clothing, a connection to the community mental health clinic, and job training. The program now has a great variety of residences, both short and long term, for many kinds of previously homeless people. Training projects include: "Back H.O.M.E. Cafe" catering to many other organizations while training its own residents; "The Cornerstone Community Book & Art Center" which provides books focusing on ecumenical, spiritual, theological, social justice, and peace issues while also employing formerly homeless persons. Some of the program's additional projects include: forty-eight units of permanent housing for men and women with special needs; Our Daily Threads Thrift Store, employment and good clothes at low cost; Seeds of Hope, an after school program for children in the neighborhood.

The Homeless Garden Project
P.O. Box 617
Santa Cruz, California 25061
Phone: 408-426-3609
This project provides space, seeds, and assistance so that homeless people can work in gardens, providing both a more beautiful environment and a place to be. The healing nature of the project is apparent to all who are involved with it.

Kidstart
Mercy Hospital
Springfield, Massachusetts
The program works with homeless preschoolers. Case workers evaluate the children and link them with Head Start or other programs, while simultaneously dealing with parental concerns. In its first year it served seventy homeless children.

Lima Small Child Welfare House
Caritas-Lima
Lima, Peru
Contact: Sr. Maria Cordoba
One of a number of programs sponsored by the archdiocese of Lima to reach out to street children, the Lima Small Child Welfare House provides shelter, nutrition, emotional and health services, vocational, recreational, and educational programs. Many Latin American countries are struggling to work with street children who are separated from families and supporting themselves in whatever way is possible.

Marseph
Chicago, Illinois
Co-sponsored by Marillac Social Center and Saint Joseph Health Center and Hospital, Marseph provides life and work skills to homeless men who visit a day shelter. Participants receive housing assistance, a uniform, transportation to the center, meal passes for the hospital cafeteria, and counseling. Jobs are initially within the health system. During the six-month program participants receive additional training and at end of the program are assisted in finding regular employment. The program is linked to a number of corporations which have hired the graduates of the program.

Mercy Housing, Inc. (MHI)
Denver, Colorado
Phone: 303-393-3755
MHI develops and operates service-enriched, multi-family rental housing for low- and very-low-income people in ten western states. Sponsored by the Auburn, Burlingame, Cedar Rapids, and Omaha communities of the Sisters of Mercy and the Sisters of St. Joseph of Peace, it has created over twelve hundred units of affordable housing since 1987. MHI's Mercy Loan Fund is capitalized with $6 million of no- or low-interest rate investments from religious congregations, and it underwrites loans for affordable housing projects, reaching 8,000 people.

Dreuding Center Project Rainbow
413 W. Master St.
Philadelphia, Pennsylvania 19122
Phone: 215-769-1830
Sr. Ellen Marvel, CSR, President & CEO
This program provides housing in small apartments for homeless women and children. Services include training programs for the women, child care during the day for pre-schoolers, and after school care for older children. The After Care Program works with 125 graduate families giving additional assistance as they move toward independence.

Transitional Living Center
3128 N. Hemlock
Spokane, Washington 99205
Phone: 509-325-2595, fax 509-325-2958
Founded by Spokane Dominican Sisters, now co-sponsored by four congregations in the area, the center provides for homeless single

women with one to three children under ten years of age. The facility has sixteen complete one- to-three bedroom apartments, providing for thirty-five to forty women and children. It provides counseling, on-site child care, basic life skills training, healthcare, transportation, education, and training. The women also receive employment-seeking and parenting skills. Staff members work in collaboration with existing social service agencies to help the women during and after their stay at the center.

POVERTY

Center of Attention
Tucson, Arizona
Director: Tommie Thomas
This is an outreach program that provides a variety of free services to at-risk youths. Operating from her home, Ms. Thomas provides recreation, education, nutrition and cultural experiences five days a week. She was also involved in starting an emergency food and clothing bank and a transportation system for seniors to get to doctors.

Childspace
Philadelphia, Pennsylvania
This worker-owned cooperative with two centers serves 235 children (in 1997), employing thirty-five staff, mainly drawn from low-income groups. The cooperative provides better-than-industry-standard compensation, as well as doing high-level training. Since all workers are also owners, they have the experience of being responsible for the success of the program, and are involved in decision making in the cooperative. The staff are encouraged and assisted in improving their education.

Connections
Pasco County, Florida
Contact: Sr. Joan Foley, MMS
Phone: 813-849-4724; 813-842-3905
A job development program, Connections brings together people who need work with companies that need employees. Staff members help unemployed people to identify their skills, work on resumes, and gain the confidence to apply for jobs; they also maintain a connection with potential employers and work with other social agencies in the county and surrounding areas.

First African Methodist Episcopal Church
Los Angeles, California
This church-based program gives low-interest loans to minority business people to help them become established in business. Simultaneously, the project helps neighborhoods where the businesses are located.

Fourth World Movement
Founded in 1957 by a French Catholic priest, the late Joseph Wresinski, this organization's belief is that the "solution to persistent poverty lies not in charity or handouts but in truly considering the poor as partners." An international movement, it has 370 full time U.S. volunteers.

Franciscan Center
2212 Maryland Avenue
Baltimore, Maryland
Director: Sr. Kathleen DeLancey, OSF
The center provides emergency services including clothing, financial assistance, groceries, and lunches. It also provides an adult literacy program and training in basic education and job skills; as a result, many of their graduates have gotten jobs.

Grameen Bank
Dhakka, Bangladesh
This bank, was established by Mohammed Yunus to offer small low-interest loans that would encourage women to start small cottage industries. The bank now has branches in half of the villages in Bangladesh. It has become an extraordinary example of trusting the poor and being rewarded, by both the success of the people and a very high rate of on-time returns of loans.

IHM Literacy Center
5th and Lindley
Philadelphia, Pennsylvania 19120
Director: Sr. Mary Ellen, IHM
This program has morning, afternoon, and evening classes to provide for the different schedules of the clients. Beyond a small registration fee, the classes are free. They include: English as a Second Language, Adult Literacy, GED preparation, and Adult Basic Education. With several full-time teachers and a large number of volunteer tutors, the center serves up to 200 adults in each session, including a summer session. The funding comes from donations from small foundations and groups. The City of Philadelphia, through its *Adult Literacy Pro-*

gram, provides materials and training workshops for all volunteers who work in this or other literacy centers.

Independent Fabrication Inc.
Dorchester, Massachusetts
An employee-owned cooperative manufacturing high performance bicycle frames used in mountain biking, this organization is committed to hiring and training low-income workers and expects to have twenty full time jobs by its fifth year of operation. It has received enthusiastic reviews in specialized biking magazines for the quality of its bicycles. Initial funding came from the U.S. Catholic Conference's *Campaign for Human Development* (see Foundations).

Keeping Kids Warm
Charming Shoppes: Fashion Bug
450 Winks Lane
Bensalem, Pennsylvania
Phone: 215-245-9100
President and CEO: Dorrit Bern
This is a corporation that has a commitment to help the neediest in the areas where its stores are located. Through the Keeping Kids Warm program it distributes new winter coats to poor children, doing it through the schools and in cooperation with the Home and School Associations. The company has eleven hundred stores in forty-five states.

The Kitchen
Springfield, Missouri
Contact: Sr. Lorraine Biebel
Services are provided for poor and homeless people. Supporters include fifty area churches, forty of them Protestant, with a $1 million grant from Housing and Urban Development. Services include meals, short-term housing in a former hotel, long-term transitional housing to eighteen families in furnished apartments, medical and dental clinics, a pharmacy, day care center, parenting and GED classes, and drug rehabilitation work with participants.

PhilaPride
1818 Market Street
Suite 3510
Philadelphia, Pennsylvania 19103-3681
Mark Viggiano, Executive Director, 215-575-2210
This non-profit organization was established in 1985 to promote a

cleaner environment and develop civic pride, especially in poorer areas. Programs include major cleanup of neighborhoods by involving both the neighbors and volunteers; a Kids for Clothes Used Clothing Drive, during which children in schools bring used clothes for needy families (25 tons in 1995); litter control and graffiti removal and landscaping, including neighborhood garden projects.

Powerful Voices
Co-sponsors: Sisters of Charity of Cincinnati, Dominican Sisters of Sinsinawa, Wisconsin
This is an exciting coalition of community-based organizations dedicated to building the political clout of low-income people, teaching them how to access the government services to which they have a right and to demand the changes needed.

St. Petersburg Free Clinic
St. Petersburg, Florida
This very large walk-in free clinic, which uses mainly volunteers, including doctors, nurses, and pharmacists, as well as legal aid lawyers, retired people, and church groups, runs a food bank, a legal aid clinic, several battered women's shelters, and an elder care resource center. The clinic reaches out to the poor of the St. Petersburg area. The clinic director has also been involved in consciousness raising among the civic, church, and political communities of St. Petersburg and of state government of Florida.

WOMEN AND CHILDREN AND VIOLENCE

1. General Programs

Barrios Unidos
313 Front St.
Santa Cruz, California 95060
Phone: 408-457-8208
This program uses community workers who have experienced and overcome the challenges facing them to work with young people and help them choose life-affirming behavior rooted in positive self-esteem, meaningful activities, and cultural pride. The program tries to bring peace to the barrio through outreach, organizing, leadership development, and job-readiness programs.

Boys and Girls Clubs of America
771 First Avenue
New York, New York 10017
Phone: 212-351-5900
Boys and Girls Clubs of America place special emphasis on inner city youth who are most susceptible to violence. Their strategies emphasize providing safe, professionally staffed environments where youth are involved in programs that develop problem-solving skills and promote healthy self-esteem and positive intra-group behavior.

Centro Sister Isolina Ferre
Ponce Playa, Puerto Rico
Originally designed to deal with juvenile delinquency, the Centro has been successful in limiting violence by actively involving and revitalizing the community. It provides educational alternatives and job training, youth and family advocacy, and a community health program.

Children of Mine Community Center
Washington, D.C.
Contact: Hannah Hawkins
A neighborhood after-school program for underprivileged children in Mrs. Hawkins's southeast Washington neighborhood of Anacostia, the center provides homework aid, assistance to children in trouble, a safe space to play, and supper each day donated by the District of Columbia Central Kitchen and Central Union Mission. It interacts with parents and teachers in providing loving support and strong but loving discipline to neighborhood children.

Educational Development Center, Inc.
55 Chapel Street
Newton, Massachusetts 02160
This organization has compiled a list of church-based and community-based programs on violence prevention.

Family Life Orientation Program
Kasanga, Uganda
Started by a parish in response to family problems related to battering and divorce, this program's activities and classes deal with responsible parenting and child care. The emphasis is on increasing personal awareness, educating for values, and leadership training. The program now has twenty centers in ten villages where it runs work-

shops on nutrition, hygiene, and disease prevention, as well as literacy programs. It encourages people to work together to improve the life of the whole community.

Freedom School Summer
Sojourners Community
2401 15th St., NW
Washington, D.C. 20009
This is an annual program run for children each summer in an inner-city D.C. neighborhood. It is connected with Children's Defense Fund/Black Student Leadership Network. Volunteers, teenagers from the neighborhood, and parents are involved in providing reading support, computer training, conflict resolution, and community service to fifty elementary and middle school children. The program offers alternatives to the violence prevalent in this section of Washington.

Incarnation Parish
5th & Lindley
Philadelphia, Pennsylvania 19120
Incarnation Parish built a gymnasium in the late 1950s for its school. Today the gym is used every evening and throughout the weekend by a variety of groups who work with teenagers and young people. The goal of the program is to use sports to encourage a reduction of violence by and among children and teenagers.

Louis Armstrong Manhood Development Program
New Orleans, Louisiana
Using an Afrocentric approach that includes African traditions of male initiation, this program teaches young African-American boys the art and science of becoming men. It functions as an extended family and community providing positive male role models for boys between the ages of eight and seventeen.

Philadelphia High School Academies, Inc.
230 S. Broad St.
Philadelphia, Pennsylvania 19102
Phone: 215-546-6300
A partnership between the public school system and area businesses, this program functions as "schools within schools," combining academic studies with occupational training in eleven career areas, e.g., communications, business, healthcare, electrical science, automotive

science. Each Academy has its own core of teachers and career-focused curriculum and provides smaller classes, incentive activities such as community service, and paid part-time and summer work experience. The Academies promote higher attendance rates, increased graduation rates, and entrance to employment or post-secondary school studies. Started in 1969, the program has helped reduce violence among teens.

P.A.L.: Police Athletic League

Active in many cities, this is a coalition of police, families, and other groups to provide after-school athletic programs for children. P.A.L. uses school and church facilities, enlists volunteers, and promotes the value of sports in the lives of children. P.A.L. fosters a healthy interconnection with police through a buddy system.

Project Spirit
The Congress of National Black Churches, Inc.
600 New Hampshire Avenue, NW
Suite 650
Washington, D.C. 20037-2403
Phone: 202-333-3060
This project serves African-American pastors, parents, and children. Strategies include after-school tutoring, living skills enhancement, and parent education.

St. Elizabeth School
801 Argonne Drive
Baltimore, Maryland
Dr. Christine Manlove, Ed.D., Principal
A non-public day school for students from eleven to twenty-one with intellectual or emotional disabilities, St. Elizabeth's provides vocational training, work experience, and programs in functional academics and social skills development.

St. Gabriel's Episcopal Church
Front St. and Roosevelt Blvd.
Philadelphia, Pennsylvania
This church started an after-school program shortly after a new pastor, Rev. Lainey, arrived several years ago. The program runs five days a week from after school until 6 P.M. The children receive assistance in doing their homework and participate in different speical programs each day.

Senior Tutors for Youth
3640 Grand Avenue
Oakland, California 94610
Phone: 415-839-1039
This program serves delinquent boys and adolescent boys and girls at a residential group center. The youngsters are mainly inner-city children with below-normal basic skills and a high danger of moving into violence. Strategies utilize elderly volunteers from a nearby retirement community, pairing one-on-one for periods of one to nine months. Pairs bond and discuss academic, social, emotional, vocational, and personal problems. Prior to each week of tutoring, volunteers receive one hour of training.

2. Values: Conflict Resolution

Caring Profile Values Modification Program
Leake and Watts Services Group Homes
New York, New York
Michael Schulman, Ph.D., Director
This program aims to help troubled adolescents replace their angry feelings toward others with gentle, empathic ones. Children are encouraged to find and re-experience the joy of loving someone, whether family or friend. The program serves one hundred troubled teenagers.

CASEL: Collaborative for the Advancement of Social and Emotional Learning
Yale Child Studies Center
P.O. Box 207900
New Haven, Connecticut 06520-7900
Mary Schwab-Stone, M.D., Director
This program works in the New Haven school system to help children develop emotional literacy skills and learn alternative ways to deal with conflict and diversity.

Community of Caring
Founded by Eunice Kennedy Shriver with funding from Joseph P. Kennedy Jr.
Foundation.
This program is used in 160 schools in twenty states and Washington, D.C. It originated as a program for pregnant teens, specifically to discourage repeat pregnancies. The focus is on teaching values and decision making to teenagers, using concepts of caring and trusting, respecting others, and respecting oneself. The program aims to create

a community within the school, so that children can live and cooperate together and develop a sense of personal discipline, belonging, and respect.

CUNAD: Community of United Neighbors Against Drugs
Philadelphia, Pennsylvania
This program, which is part of the Weed and Seed Project, is run by a group in North Philadelphia. The program works to promote a safe neighborhood, free of drugs and crime, by providing workshops for children age six to seventeen. The workshops, which are facilitated by Justserve Americorp members, deal with leadership skills, drug and alcohol prevention, AIDS awareness, and social skills.

Educators for Social Responsibility Conflict Resolution Programs
23 Garden St.
Cambridge, Massachusetts 02138
Phone: 617-492-1764
This program serves teachers, administrators, counselors, and parents by offering programs, workshops, curriculum, and resources dealing with alternative ways to handle various forms of violence and conflict.

Harvard Negotiation Project
Building Bridges
Harvard Law School
Pound Hall, Room 513
Cambridge, Massachusetts 02138
Phone: 617-495-1684
This project primarily serves high school students and teachers by providing a peer-taught curriculum on effective handling of conflict. While providing a framework for the peaceful resolution of social and international conflict, it is primarily geared toward those inner-city and suburban youth who are most vulnerable to violence.

Peace Camp
St. Mary Hospital
Franciscan Health System of New Jersey
Hoboken, New Jersey
St. Mary Hospital runs a week-long Peace Camp for children. At the camp children learn how to prevent violence and are encouraged to find effective and peaceful solutions to problems. The program was started in response to the health system's recognition that violence

was a health problem reaching epidemic proportions throughout the country, in both urban and suburban areas (55 percent of suburban children responded in a study done by Search Institute on Middle America that they had engaged in violence). Children learn alternative ways of dealing with anger and frustration by using role playing, discussions, and skits that emphasize the positive approaches.

Peacemakers Program of Conflict Resolution
Public School 321
Brooklyn, New York
This integrated school in the Park Slope section of Brooklyn has a "Peacemakers" program of conflict resolution. Children as young as five learn how to assert themselves and their rights without triggering aggressive responses. "The lessons of assertion and civility are taught formally and then incorporated into the daily life of the classroom …children who learn to assert themselves without verbally or physically attacking others are not only less likely to become bullies, they are also less likely to become the victims of bullies. Mediation is the second component…children are elected by their classmates and trained to negotiate settlements when disputes break out among their peers…peer mediation at the high school level is known to reduce fighting and reduce suspensions and expulsions."

Philadelphia Injury Prevention Program
Medical Examiners Office
321 University Avenue, 2nd floor
Philadelphia, Pennsylvania 19131
Strategies are built around community safe blocks, where homes on each block are visited and interventions are initiated. A school-based violence curriculum is also part of the program. A post-intervention program takes place in a major hospital where victims of violence are counseled.

Teaching Tolerance
Southern Poverty Law Center
400 Washington Ave.
Montgomery, Alabama 35104
Morris Dees, National Chairman
This program, which aims to curb the rising tide of racial tension and violence, reaches over fifty thousand schools and three million students. It won an Oscar for its documentary film. The video is sent free to schools which request it. The center also provides teaching

kits which include the video, for grades K thru 12, and a magazine is sent free twice a year to two hundred thousand teachers.

Urban Development Initiative
2020 Pennsylvania Ave., NW
Washington, D.C. 20006
Phone: 202-293-0297
In July 1995, the Urban Youth Summit brought together young people from Philadelphia, Louisville, Milwaukee, Bridgeport, and Washington, D.C. to learn how to develop ways of reducing violence in their cities through conflict resolution, community organizing, and diversity awareness. The young people developed strategies to take back to their own cities for combating violence and addressing the root causes of poverty, teen pregnancy, drugs and alcohol.

The Violence Prevention Curriculum for Adolescents
Educational Development Corporation
Newton, Massachusetts
This is a curriculum developed to help people who want to work in the area of prevention of violence among and directed toward adolescents. It can be used by parents as well as teachers and administrators.

3. Residential Programs

Casa de los Niños
Tucson, Arizona
A non-profit, nonsectarian residential care shelter for children who are abused, neglected, or homeless, the Casa also provides supportive counseling to families. Staff members are involved in community education, serving as advocates for children. The Casa is also a 24-hour emergency shelter for children from infancy through age eleven.

4. Healthcare Programs: Violence Prevention

CHAMPS: Comprehensive Health and Medical Preventive Services
Fitzgerald Mercy Hospital and Mercy Health Corporation
Darby, Pennsylvania
Contact: Sr. Donna M. Watto, RSM, 610-237-4895
This program is directed toward reducing and eliminating violence through preventive healthcare initiatives. CHAMPS provides pediatric healthcare services in area schools and day care centers. It offers immunizations, vision screening, dental care, and physical exams.

Domestic Violence Task Force
Sacred Heart Medical Center
Spokane, Washington
Contact: Deborah Markin, R.N., 509-455-4619
The program was started to educate hospital personnel to recognize signs of domestic violence. It helps teachers and organizations, such as the police department and HMOs, to identify and treat victims of domestic violence. It has also published a brochure that advises battered women on how to leave an abusive situation.

Hospital Response to Community Violence: HRCV
St. Louis University Hospital
St. Louis, Missouri
A Level I trauma center, located in a poor downtown area, HRCV has a two-pronged approach to the violence in its environment: (1) several educational activities to spread the message of nonviolence to school children and populations at risk of becoming violent offenders; (2) holistic, ongoing support and education for hospitalized trauma victims. HRCV also sponsors educational workshops for parents and an annual Christmas party at local public schools to have children reflect on how they can contribute to peace in the world, and a toy gun buy-back program. The staff members work with patients who are victims of recurring violence. The program has also been successful in helping some teenagers move away from violence.

Providence Holy Cross Medical Center
Violence Prevention Program
Mission Hills, California
The goals of this program are to increase community awareness in order to decrease violence; to provide violence prevention programs in the schools; and to develop a community coalition to collaborate on violence prevention. Community agencies, law enforcement, schools, youth groups, churches, and businesses regularly meet together. The program brings together social workers and ex-gang members to offer alternatives to hospital patients who may be involved with gangs.

Teen Heartline for Help
St. Joseph Medical Center
Wichita, Kansas
Contact: Kit Lambertz, 316-689-6259
The Medical Center organized a week of intensive training on how to

help teens affected by gangs, violence, suicide, and pregnancy, then established a 24-hour hotline and advertised on billboards and the local MTV station. The hotline uses both volunteers and professional back-up support persons to talk to the teens and give them immediate counseling and information.

"Trauma Care"
St. Vincent Medical Center
Toledo, Ohio
A Level I trauma center in the central city area, Trauma Care treats most of the youthful victims of violent crime. An interdisciplinary team of people from the hospital, the city, and the local high school developed "Kids Saving Kids," a dramatization which shows teens what happens when someone is injured by a penetrating weapon. The program, which also introduces teens to alternative nonviolent behaviors, is now being used in the schools and the plan is to move it into recreation centers.

Youth Services/Family Focus Center
St. Bernardine Medical Center
San Bernardino, California
Contact: Linda McDonald, 909-883-8711, ext. 3525
This service offers a network of community resources: a parenting program, late night basketball leagues, job training and mentoring, a teen support group, an image/attitude program, counseling, and a resource/referral library.

REFERENCES

Many of the ideas in this book have come from my experience, while others are the fruit of my long habit of reading. I want to give credit to the many authors who have influenced my thinking, even if they are not directly cited in the book.

"Appropriate Technology." In *Medical Mission Sisters News*, v. 22, no. 1, 1992.

Bellah, Robert N. "Healing in an Ailing Society." Address to the Catholic Health Association, Annual Assembly, June 14, 1992.

Bernardin, Joseph. *A Sign of Hope: a Pastoral Letter on Healthcare.* Chicago: Archdiocese of Chicago Office of Communications, 1995.

Block, F., R. A. Cloward, B. Ehrenreich, F. F. Piven. *The Mean Season: the Attack on the Welfare State.* New York: Pantheon Books, 1987.

Boff, Clodovis, and George V. Pixley. *The Bible, the Church, and the Poor.* Maryknoll, New York: Orbis Books, 1986.

Bonnyman, Gordon. "The Healing Game." In *Sojourners*, v. 24, no. 5, 1995, pp. 30-31.

———. "Moral Malpractice." In *Sojourners*, v. 25, no. 3, 1996, pp. 12-17.

Borg, Marcus J. *Meeting Jesus Again for the First Time: The Historical Jesus and the Heart of Contemporary Faith.* San Francisco: Harper Collins, 1995.

Casey, Juliana, IHM. *Food for the Journey: Theological Foundations of the Catholic Healthcare Ministry.* St. Louis: Catholic Health Association, 1991.

———. "Suffering and Dying with Dignity." In Francis A. Eigo, ed. *Suffering and Healing in Our Day.* Villanova, Pennsylvania: Villanova University Press, p. 139.

Clinton, Hillary Rodham. *It Takes a Village: And Other Lessons Children Teach Us.* New York: Simon & Schuster, 1996.

CMSM/LCWR Task Force. *A Vision of Life, Health, Sickness, and Death for Religious.* Silver Spring, Maryland: LCWR, 1995.

Collins, Chuck, and Felice Yeskel. "The Growing Gap Between the Rich...and Everybody Else." In *Network*, v. 24, no. 3, 1996.

Crowley, Susan L. "Children Under Siege: Marian Wright Edelman Fights to Keep Hard-Won Benefits." In *AARP Bulletin*, v. 37, no. 6, 1996, p.16.

Donaher, Kevin, ed. *50 years Is Enough*. Boston: South End Press, 1994.

Drinan, Robert F. "Congress Poised to Clip Poor, Aid Big Biz." In *National Catholic Reporter*, v. 32, no. 11, 1996, p. 18.

———. "Injustice Bared: Corporate Welfare Thrives." In *National Catholic Reporter*, v. 32, no. 12, 1996, p. 29.

Edelman, Marian Wright. "Who's Responsible for America's Children? In *Network*, v. 24, no. 3, 1996, pp. 10-11.

Edwards, Robin T. "Hannah Hawkins: In Her Haven, She Nurtures, Disciplines her 'Sheep.'" In *National Catholic Reporter*, v. 31, no. 33, 1995, pp. 6-7.

Etzioni, Amitai. *The Spirit of Community: Rights, Responsibilities, and the Communitarian Agenda*. New York: Crown, 1993.

Farren, Suzy. "This Ain't a Game, It's Life or Death." In *Catholic Health World*, Special Assembly Issue, 1996, pp. 1, 4.

Ferre, M. Isolina. "Prevention and Control of Violence through Community Revitalization, Individual Dignity, and Personal Self-Confidence." In *Annals, ASPSS*, #494, November 1987, pp. 27-36.

Foley, Joan. "Bringing Heart into Helping People Find Jobs." In *Inter-Continent*, no. 216, July 1996, pp. 20-21.

Fox, Tom. "Military Funds—53 Percent and Growing." In *National Catholic Reporter*, v. 33, no. 2, 1996, p. 2.

Gallegos, Aaron. "Voices of Experience: Urban Youth Create Plans to Counter Violence." In *Sojourners*, v. 24, no. 4, 1995, p. 43.

Gans, Herbert J. *The War Against the Poor: the Underclass and Antipoverty Policy*. New York: Basic Books, 1995.

Giamo, Benedict, and Jeffrey Grunberg. *Beyond Homelessness: Frames of Reference*. Iowa City: University of Iowa Press, 1992.

Golden, Stephanie. *The Women Outside: Meanings and Myths of Homelessness*. Berkeley: University of California Press, 1992.

Gootee, Pat. "Battered Lives, Family Pain." In *InterContinent*, no. 209, April 1994, pp. 8-9.

"Group Notes Abortion Increase." In *National Catholic Reporter*, v. 33, no. 3, 1996, p. 10.

"Growing Up Too Fast: Teens Having Babies..." In *Community Focus*, Spring/Summer, 1996, pp. 6-9.

Harman, Willis W. "Premises, Premises: A Tale of Conflicting Assumptions." In *AHP Perspectives*, September-October, 1995, pp. 14-15.

———. "Toward a New Eco-nomics: A Whole-System View." In *Noetic Sciences Review*, Autumn, 1994, pp. 24-31.

Harmer, Catherine M. *Religious Life in the 21st Century: A Contemporary Journey into Canaan.* Mystic, Connecticut: Twenty-Third Publications, 1995.

Hart, Stephen. *What Does the Lord Require? How American Christians Think About Economic Justice.* New York: Oxford University Press, 1992.

Holmes, George R. *Helping Teenagers into Adulthood: A Guide for the Next Generation.* Westport, Connecticut: Praeger, 1995.

Hug, Jim. "The War on the Poor." In *Center Focus*, Issue #130, 1996, pp. 1-6.

"Hunger Increases in U.S., Africa." In *National Catholic Reporter*, v. 33, no. 2, 1996, p. 8.

Inlander, Charles B. "Managing Care?" In *Peoples' Medical Society Newsletter*, v. 15, no. 5., 1996, p. 2.

Islam: The Qur'an. Tr. Ahmed Ali. Princeton, New Jersey: Princeton University Press, 1988.

Jacobs, Jane. *Cities and the Wealth of Nations.* New York: Random House, 1984.

Johnson, Rachel. "Growing Hope." In *Sojourners*, v. 24, no. 4, 1995, p. 44.

John Paul II. *Sollicitudo Rei Socialis.* In *Origins*, v. 17, no. 38, 1988, pp. 641-660.

Johnston, Charles M. *Necessary Wisdom: Meeting the Challenge of a New Cultural Maturity.* Seattle: ICD Press, 1991.

Joseph, James A. *Remaking America: How the Benevolent Traditions of Many Cultures Are Transforming Our National Life.* San Francisco, Jossey-Bass, 1995.

Kaithakary, Jane Mary. "The Family Life Orientation Program." In *InterContinent*, no. 209, April 1994, pp. 9-11.

Kozol, Jonathan. *Amazing Grace: The Lives of Children and the Conscience of a Nation.* New York: Crown, 1995.

"Legislating Responsibility: A Proposal." In *Harper's Magazine*, v. 292, no. 1752, 1996, p. 45.

Lietaer, Bernard A. "Is a Community Currency Just Another Welfare System?" In *AHP Perspective*, September-October 1995, p. 23.

Mann, Peter, and Jenifer Urff. "The Future of Work—Strategies for Change." In *Network Connection*, September/October, 1995, pp. 3-5.

Marty, Martin E. "Can We Still Hear the Call?" In *Health Progress*, v. 76, no. 1, pp. 18-21.

McNeal, Gloria J. "High-tech Mobile Healthcare." In *SePaScope*, v. xvi, no. 1, 1996.

———. "Mobile Health Care for Those at Risk." In *N&HC: Perspectives on Community*, v. 17, no. 3, 1996, pp. 134-140.

"Mercies Aim to Increase Rate of Women Homeowners." In *Catholic Health World*, v. 12, no. 14, 1996, p. 2.

Millennium: Confronting Urban Health Challenges: Urban Health Challenges for the 21st Century. Sterling, Virginia: Inmed, 1994.

Miller, Amata. "Needed: Citizenship for the Common Good." In *Network Connection*, v. 22, no. 5, 1994, pp. 3-5.

————. "Winds of Challenge: Calls from Our World." Talk given at LCWR National Assembly, August 27, 1994.

Mincy, Ronald B., ed. *Nurturing Young Black Males.* Washington, D.C.: Urban Institute, 1994.

Murphy, Peter J. "A Renaissance in Healthcare?" In *Health Progress*, v. 76, no. 1, 1995, p. 30-31, 53.

Murray, Bridget. "Getting By with a Little Help from Some Friends." In *Monitor*, v. 27, no. 1, 1996, p. 41.

Niebuhr, Reinhold. *Man's Nature and His Communities: Essays on the Dynamics and Enigmas of Man's Personal and Social Existence.* New York: Charles Scribner's Sons, 1965.

"On the Front Lines of the Periphery." In *Catholic Health World*, v. 12, no. 10, 1995, pp. 4-5.

O'Rourke, Kevin D., OP. "Making Mission Possible." In *Health Progress*, v. 76, no. 6, 1995, pp. 45-47, 60.

Palmer, Parker. *The Company of Strangers: Christians and the Renewal of America's Public Life.* New York: Crossroad, 1981.

Pinkerton, Catherine, CSJ. "The Canadian System: A Model for U.S. Health Care Reform?" In *Network Connection*, v. 19, no. 5, 1991, pp. 3-5.

Prothrow-Stith, Deborah, with Michaele Weissman. *Deadly Consequences: How Violence Is Destroying Our Teenage Population and a Plan to Begin Solving the Problem.* New York: HarperCollins, 1991.

Reich, Robert B. *Tales of a New America.* New York: Times Books, 1987.

Rochette, Madeleine, CND. "The Prophetic Dimension of Apostolic Religious Life." In *UISG Bulletin*, no. 95, 1995, pp. 57-59.

Schorr, Lisbeth B. "Successful Health Programs for the Poor and Underserved." In *Journal of Health Care for the Poor and Underserved*, v. 1, no. 3, 1990, pp. 271-277.

Semple, David M. "From Ministry to Market." In *Health Progress*, v. 77, no. 5, 1996, pp. 18-24.

Solomon, Robert C. *A Passion for Justice: Emotions and the Origins of the Social Contract.* Reading, Massachusetts: Addison-Wesley, 1990.

"Some Want the Poor Punished for Lack of Success." In *National Catholic Reporter*, v. 32, no. 11, 1995, p. 24.

Stubbs, Mary Louise, DC. "Violence: Ripping the Fabric of Society." In *Health Progress*, v. 77, no. 2, 1996, pp. 25-40. (Special section on violence.)

Theobald, Robert. *Turning the Century: Personal and Organizational Strategies for Your Changed World.* Indianapolis: Knowledge Systems, 1992.

Thornton, Kathy. "Political Education in the Windy City." In *Network*, v. 23, no. 1, 1995.

Timmer, Doug A., et al. *Paths to Homelessness: Extreme Poverty and the Urban Housing Crisis.* Boulder, Colorado: Westview Press, 1994.

"United Nations Expert Group on Women and Finance." New York: Women's World Banking, 1994.

Wallis, Jim. "A Great National Sin." In *Sojourners*, v. 25, no. 5, 1996, p. 7.

———. "Lift Every Voice." In *Sojourners*, v. 25, no. 4, 1996, pp. 7-8.

———. "Which Future Will We Choose?" In *Sojourners*, v. 24, no. 4, 1995, p. 6.

———. *The Soul of Politics: A Practical and Prophetic Vision for Change.* New York: The New Press and Orbis Books, 1994.

Warmoth, Arthur. "The Metropolitan Bioregion as a Political and Economic Unit." In *AHP Perspective*, September-October, 1995, pp. 20-21.

Weakland, Rembert G. "Hear the Cries of the Poor: the Urban Poor and the Churches." Speech given Oct. 17, 1996, at National Pastoral Life Center Urban Ministries Conference. (Excerpts in *National Catholic Reporter*, v. 33, no. 2, p. 9.)